decorating *tricks*

FOR
CHRISTMAS

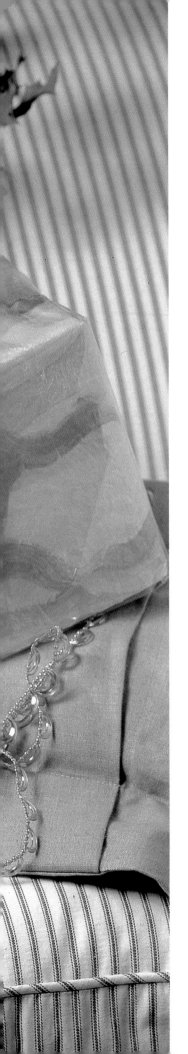

decorating *tricks*

FOR
CHRISTMAS

Rubena Grigg

Over 60 seasonal ideas for
the festive period

hamlyn

First published in Great Britain in 2000 by Hamlyn
an imprint of Octopus Publishing Group Ltd
2–4 Heron Quays, London E14 4JP

© Octopus Publishing Group Ltd 2000

Distributed in the United States and Canada by
Sterling Publishing Co., Inc
387 Park Avenue South
New York, NY 10016-8810

Commissioning Editor NINA SHARMAN
Editor KATEY DAY
Project Editor JO LETHABY
Art Director KEITH MARTIN
Designer MIKE MOULE
Senior Designer LOUISE GRIFFITHS
Production Controller LOUISE HALL

Photography DI LEWIS
Illustrator CARRIE HILL

A CIP record for this book is available from the
British Library.

ISBN 0 600 59835 7

The publishers have made every effort to ensure that
all instructions given in this book are accurate and
safe, but they cannot accept liability for any resulting
injury, damage or loss to either person or property
whether direct or consequential and howsoever
arising. The author and publishers will be grateful for
any information that will assist them in keeping
future editions up to date.

Printed and bound in China

Contents

Introduction

Traditionally, Christmas is a great family occasion, a time of coming together, of visiting and entertaining. For many families this is still the case. However, it has also become a particularly stressful and expensive time.

Christmas can be wonderfully magical if you have small children in the house, but for several years, with only adults around, it rather lost its appeal for me. All the excitement in the preparation and cooking for Christmas seemed to be only during the weeks leading up to the big day, which in itself became more of an anti-climax. However, with the presence now of grandchildren old enough to understand the meaning of Christmas, and with whom it is enjoyable and fun to gather autumn leaves for pressing and drying, and fir cones, seed heads and sea shells for decorating, it is once again an exciting and inspiring time. Children adore making their own presents with particular family members and friends in mind and they will enjoy helping you make some of the projects in this book.

The trick I have discovered is to be more disciplined and organized and not to be brow-beaten by all the "hype" into dashing around crowded shops and department stores, time and time again, looking for presents – sometimes any present! – at great expense. Instead, take a few minutes to make a list of special friends or members of the family who would really appreciate a truly original handmade gift. How lovely to make something especially for someone, knowing their interests and hobbies – a unique gift that will be greatly appreciated, and used, rather than a box of chocolates, a jar of bath salts or a plant to wither and die. Similarly, don't waste your time, money and energy looking for very ordinary cards and wrapping paper, when you could relax at home and enjoy two or three evenings designing and making your own. People always enjoy receiving cards that have been handmade by friends or children, who have taken the time and effort to make something absolutely unique.

Draw up a comprehensive list of basic "ingredients" you will need for your chosen projects and make one or two forays to your nearest craft supplier, or send for their mail order catalogue (see page 142) and choose at home. In addition, keep your eyes open for other items. Always consider the potential use of remnants of ribbon and fabric, an old cake frill, a few sequins or beads, shells and pretty stones, or a broken necklace or earrings. Whenever you have the chance during the year, scour charity shops, antiques markets or local jumble sales for pretty fabrics, unusual buttons, lampshade frames, jewellery, glassware of every description, lovely baskets, picture frames and candle holders. Believe it or not, it can become compulsive and be exciting! You will find yourself becoming squirrel-like, hoarding all these bits and bobs for future use – a real treasure trove at Christmas time!

There are plenty of natural materials worth collecting, too. Tiny larch cones appear in many of the projects in this book, as do pressed dried leaves, which you can easily collect yourself during a dry spell in late autumn. Press the leaves between the pages of a substantial book, and check after a few weeks that the leaves are dry.

Decorating Tricks for Christmas contains a wealth of the most colourful, unusual and inspiring projects for you to make for very little outlay – mainly your time. Over 60 projects are grouped into chapters to give you a rough indication of the time each may need. Since most projects are designed to give fantastic results with the minimum of effort, a hot glue gun is an absolute must for your own Christmas list if you do not already own one. No other special tools or equipment are necessary. A sewing machine would be useful and saves time, but needle and thread are just as good.

This informative and practical book contains clear step-by-step photographs and instructions to guide you through each project, and it is deliberately a little different from the traditional red, green and gold Christmassy look we have all adopted over recent years. Enjoy the book, have fun and Happy Christmas!

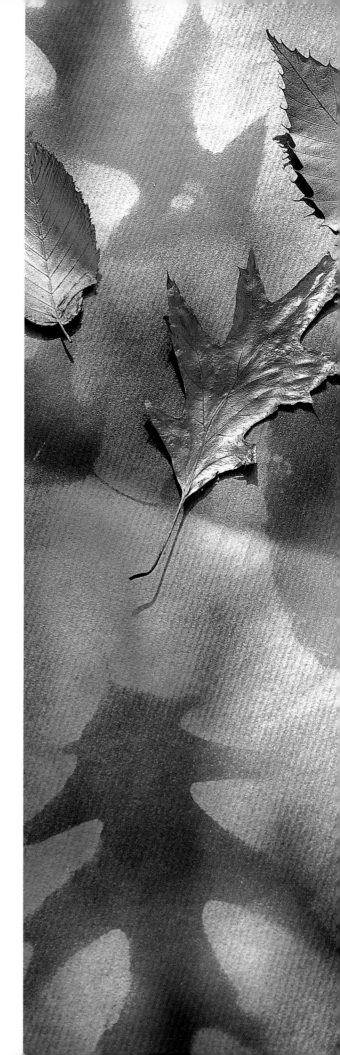

One-hour wonders

Be thrifty and inventive and have fun combining natural materials – dried leaves, sea shells, larch cones, feathers, seed heads and hedgerow vines – with metallic sprays, crystal beads, gold tissue paper and remnants of fabric to create these projects in no time at all.

Sensationally simple tree decorations

Shimmering silver and crystal both reflect the light and, offset against the dark background of a tree, they add to the magic of Christmas. Fir cones, nuts, seed heads and pressed dried leaves are also perfect for spraying with silver and gold metallic sprays, and turning into tree decorations.

LEAF AND SHELL DECORATIONS

You will need

Can of florist's silver metallic spray paint
Assorted natural materials, such as fir cones, pressed dried leaves, shells, nuts and seed heads
Hot glue gun and glue stick
Silver silk cord
Thin white cord, fine ribbon or string

Sea shells are readily available from craft suppliers if you haven't collected your own.

1. Working in a well-ventilated area, take the can of metallic spray paint in silver or another metallic colour of your choice and shake it well for a couple of minutes before beginning. Spray all the natural materials – fir cones, pressed dried leaves shells or seed heads – back and front, with paint, and remember to keep shaking the can between spraying. Allow the sprayed items to dry thoroughly.

2. Using the hot glue gun, attach three or four sprayed fir cones to the base of a large sprayed leaf or leaves. Hot glue a short length of silver cord to the back of the

decoration. Similarly, hot glue more lengths of silver cord to the backs of the sprayed shells.

3. Sprayed nuts or seed heads could be attached with glue to very fine ribbon or white string, tied into a small bow at the point of attachment to mask the blob of glue required.

CRYSTAL DECORATIONS

Old crystal bead necklaces or earrings can be unthreaded and used here or, if you cannot find real glass crystals, buy plastic equivalents from a craft supplier. These usually come as three different shapes, joined together with wire, which can be removed.

Beading needles are longer than ordinary sewing needles and fine enough to pass through tiny holes in beads. They are available from bead or craft suppliers and good needlework shops. Silver embroidery thread makes an attractive loop.

First decide on the arrangement of each crystal decoration. Thread the beading needle with silver embroidery thread and pass the needle through the holes in the top and/or bottom of each crystal as appropriate, leaving lengths of embroidery thread in between.

Thread small silver, crystal or even coloured beads on to the embroidery thread between each crystal if liked, before passing a length of silver embroidery thread through the hole in the next crystal.

To secure the thread once you have joined a pair of crystals – with or without beads in

between – overwrap the thread through the hole once or twice, then sew through a loop stitch several times. Trim the thread.

To hang each decoration, pass a 6in (15cm) length of embroidery thread through the hole in the top of each uppermost crystal. Tie the two loose ends together with a firm knot. Trim the loose ends of thread; the decoration is now ready for hanging.

TWIGGY & DRIED FRUIT DECORATIONS

You can make natural-looking decorations using hops or honey-suckle vines, cut into short lengths with secateurs and woven and coiled into rough circular shapes. In addition to these free materials that can be gathered from the wild, more unusual seed heads and small twiggy rings and balls can be purchased from large craft suppliers. Leave them as they are or spray them with florist's silver, gold or white metallic spray paint. Simply add lengths of ordinary or green garden string, raffia or narrow brightly coloured ribbon tied into little bows, and

you can easily transform them into attractive decorations for the Christmas tree.

For the dried fruit decorations above, cut oranges, lemons or pink ruby grapefruit (pictured here) into thin slices. Arrange on baking trays and place in a very low temperature oven, 120°C (250°F), Gas Mark ½, to dry out. Leave for about 1½ hours, turning them over halfway through "cooking", until the rind is hard yet the fruit retains its colour. Pierce a hole in each, thread with string and hang on the tree.

Decorated manila giftwrap & bags

Bags or sheets of brown manila paper decorated with feathers, seed heads, larch cones, shells and dried flowers or with dried spices from your kitchen cupboard such as star anise and cinnamon sticks, is a unique and attractive way of presenting gifts.

ZIGZAG MANILA GIFTWRAP

You will need

Scissors
1 sheet of brown manila paper
Hot glue gun and glue stick
Pinking shears or paper edge-cutters
Jute string or natural raffia
Natural decorations, such as shells,
*   feathers, or dried plant material*

It is easier to decorate the brown paper if it is wrapped around a regular shape so, if your gift to be wrapped is an awkward shape, try and find a suitable box in which can fit snugly.

1. Cut a strip, about 2in (5cm) wide, from one end of the sheet of brown paper. Wrap the box in the remaining paper, using hot glue to secure the ends.

2. Use the pinking shears or edge-cutters on the long sides of the strip of brown paper to give it frilly edges. Fold the strip widthways into pleats.

3. Cut out simple rounded, oval or triangular shaped holes in the centre of alternate folds of the strip of paper through which the string or raffia can be threaded.

4. Open out the pleated paper, thread the string or raffia through the holes and tie it around the brown paper-wrapped gift. Ease out the pleating along the string or raffia until it is fairly even.

5. To finish, stick your chosen decorations in place on the wrapped gift, using hot glue.

MANILA BAGS

Collect and save plain brown bags acquired on shopping trips, and keep them ready for decorating with an assortment of items. Use materials gathered from the wild – in their natural state or sprayed with metallic gold, silver or white – as well as gold foil from sweet wrappers, printed paper and jute string.

1. Decide on a design for one or both sides of the bag, accumulate all the decorative bits and heat up the glue gun.

2. Apply your chosen decorations in layers, starting with the flat materials such as printed paper, foil papers or pressed dried leaves. Take care placing the leaves – once they are in position any attempt to move them will tear the delicate dried leaf. Jute string makes an effective decoration, when cut into short lengths and glued in coils or other striking designs on the bag.

3. Allow the glue to dry then fill the bags and tie the handles together with pretty ribbon.

Silk ribbon roses

Beautiful, wire-edged ribbons that have one colour blending into another lend themselves particularly well to this project. Ribbon roses can be used to decorate gifts, mirrors or picture frames, to trim hatboxes, or in flower arrangements. They are very simple to make once you learn the knack.

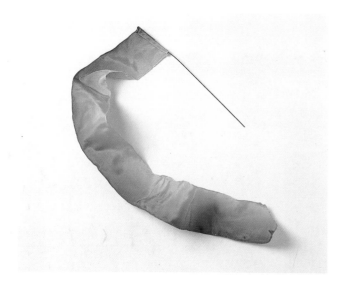

You will need

Scissors
Colour-shaded, 1½–2in (4–5cm) wide, wire-edged ribbon
Lengths of green florist's wire (stems)
Sewing needle and thread
Self-adhesive green florist's tape (optional)
Fabric rose leaves

Fabric rose leaves are available from florist's, craft suppliers or department stores. They usually come with a wire stem of 3–4in (8–10cm).

1. Cut the ribbon into lengths, allowing at least 24in (60cm) ribbon per rose.

2. Take a length of ribbon and a wire stem and align one end of the ribbon with one end of the wire stem, about 1in (2.5cm) down from the top of the wire. Wrap the ribbon tightly around the wire stem a few times. Bend the protruding 1in (2.5cm) of wire over itself to hold the ribbon in place and secure the ribbon with a few small stitches.

3. Continue wrapping the ribbon loosely around the wire, twisting it regularly and folding it back one way, then the other, to look like rose petals, always pinching it in at the base of the rose and holding it there.

4. When the rose is the size you require, secure the ribbon at the base of the flower with small neat stitches, pushing the needle right through the centre of all the layers of ribbon once or twice to secure perfectly.

5. For a professional, more attractive finish, bind green florist's tape around the first 1in (2.5cm) or so of the base of the wire stem. If adding a fabric leaf to the rose, lay the wire of the leaf stem against that of the flower and continue binding, wrapping the tape tightly around both stems as one.

Leaf-printed wrapping paper

For these wrapping papers you need to collect attractively shaped, undamaged fallen leaves in autumn when they are dry. Oak, chestnut, beech, hazel and American red oak are the easiest to find; you might have maple leaves in your own garden or decide to pick evergreen leaves such as ivy, which will take longer to dry out.

SILVER-SPRAYED LEAF PAPER

You will need

Large cardboard box
1 sheet of brown manila paper
Selection of pressed dried leaves (see below)
Can of florist's silver metallic spray paint
Pair of lightweight disposable gloves

To press leaves flat, place several at a time between the pages of a substantial book, placing sheets of paper either side of the leaves so as not to mark the pages. Close the book and weight it down with more books piled on top. After a few weeks check that the leaves are dry.

Packets of sheets of brown paper are often cheapest when purchased from a good stationer's or newsagent's as opposed to craft suppliers.

1. Make a "spray booth" by standing a large cardboard box on one side outside on a calm

day, or in a shed or some other well-ventilated space. Spread out the sheet of brown paper on an even, clean surface inside the "spray booth".

2. Arrange the pressed dried leaves on the surface of the brown paper in a pattern.

3. Take the can of spray paint and shake it well for a couple of minutes before beginning, and remember to keep shaking it in between spraying. Wear the disposable gloves so that you can hold the tips of the stems to stop the leaves blowing away when you spray them. Hold each leaf in place as you spray over it; the weight of the wet paint will eventually hold them down. Once the whole sheet of paper has been sprayed silver, leave it to dry.

4. Remove the leaves from the paper but keep them for decorating future projects. You now have a sheet of attractive and original wrapping paper ready for use.

PEWTER PAINTED LEAF PAPER

You will need

1 sheet of brown manila paper
Selection of pressed dried leaves
Jam jar with lid
Artist's acrylic tube paint in pewter
Small paintbrush
Small rubber printing roller
   (optional)

1. Spread out the sheet of brown paper. Arrange the dried leaves on the surface of the paper in a pleasing pattern.

2. Fill the jam jar with water and squeeze a little pewter paint on the jar lid, using it as a palette.

Remove one leaf from its position and decide which side you prefer to paint – the underside will show the veining better. Dip a small paintbrush in a little water, then apply the pewter paint all over one side of the leaf.

3. Return the leaf to its position on the brown paper and press firmly yet carefully to avoid smudging, using your fingertips or a rubber roller if you have one. Remove the leaf from the paper to reveal a lovely pewter imprint.

4. Continue in the same way, working with one leaf at a time, until the whole sheet is covered in pewter leaves. Leave the paper to dry thoroughly; save the leaves for decorating other projects.

GOLD TISSUE LEAF PAPER

You will need

Selection of pressed dried
   leaves
1 sheet of gold tissue paper
Pencil
Scissors
1 sheet of brown manila paper
Paper glue

1. Lay the leaves, one by one, on the back of the gold tissue paper, and draw around each one using a pencil.

2. Carefully cut out each leaf shape using sharp scissors.

3. Spread out the sheet of brown paper on a flat surface. When sufficient gold leaf shapes have been cut out, arrange them in a pleasing pattern on the brown paper.

4. Remove the gold tissue cut-outs from the brown paper one at a time and apply glue to the back of each one. Paste the cut-outs into place on the brown paper. Smooth each one flat and leave the glue to dry.

Glamorous giftbags

Festive giftbags look particularly attractive and are ideal for holding small gifts for each person at the Christmas table. Alternatively, make up enticing little bags of fabric to hang on the tree and fill with sugared almonds or foil-wrapped chocolates.

GILDED GOLD TISSUE GIFTBAGS

You will need

Scissors
Sheets of gold tissue paper
Stick adhesive
Few sheets of Dutch metal transfer leaf
Ribbon
Gift tag (optional)

If you are using these gold-coloured bags decoratively on the table you could also transform other small decorative items such as walnuts, seed heads, cape gooseberry pods or fir cones by spraying them with gold metallic spray paint or rubbing them with gilt cream, and dotting them around the table for effect.

1. For each bag, cut the gold tissue paper into two squares about 6 x 6in (15 x 15cm) or cut a rectangle 12–14in (30–35cm) x 6in (15cm) and fold in half.

2. Glue together the edges – two or three, depending on how you have cut the tissue – with a thin line of stick adhesive, leaving one side unstuck for the bag opening. When the sides are stuck, apply some glue over a smaller square

area on the front of the bag, and apply a square of transfer leaf. Leave to dry.

3. To finish the bag, cut the top in a decorative scalloped pattern. Fill the bag with goodies and tie a pretty ribbon around it, adding a gift tag if liked.

GOSSAMER GIFTBAGS

You will need

Scissors
Small piece of gold-coloured
*   metallic sheer fabric*
Long glass-headed pins
*   (optional)*
Sewing needle
Gold metallic embroidery
*   thread*
Small piece of clear cellophane
Plastic crystal or bead

There are many shimmering, fine, filigree fabrics now available, ranging from silk organza to the finest metallic fabric – all of which are perfect for making pretty little giftbags. These gold-coloured gossamer bags are "lined" with a piece of cellophane folded in half, purely for effect.

1. Cut the fabric into a rectangle. Fold it in half, right sides together and pin in place. Sew the two side seams by hand, using the gold metallic embroidery thread.

2. Turn under the top edge of the bag twice to prevent the fabric fraying; stitch in place. Turn the bag the right side out.

3. Take a piece of cellophane the same size as the fabric and fold it in half. Place it inside the bag and fill the bag with foil-wrapped chocolates. Wind more gold thread around the top of the bag to seal it, allowing extra for a loop by which to hang the bag as a tree decoration, if liked. Thread a plastic crystal or bead on to the gold thread for a finishing touch.

NET SWEETIE BAGS

White netting is another material particularly suitable for making little attractive festive bags, to be filled with sugared almonds or gold and silver foil-wrapped chocolates and hung on the Christmas tree.

For each bag, cut a small rectangle of frosty white netting. Bend it in half and sew along the side seams with silver metallic embroidery thread – since netting does not fray, the edges can be left raw. Thread the silver through the top of the bag to draw up the opening.

Last-minute gifts

These make ideal presents for the last-minute unexpected guest. Candles are always a welcome gift, while bookmarks are useful presents. Another option is to make the stunning gold cracker overleaf and fill it with delicious edible goodies, a small bottle of liqueur or fabulous "smellies" for the bath.

BUNDLES OF CANDLES

You will need

Assorted bundles of 3–6 tapered or straight candles, of any length and matching in shape and colour
Rubber bands
Scissors
Assorted ribbons, wire-edged or otherwise, or small remnants of attractive fabric and/or corrugated card
Hot glue gun and glue stick
Decorative additions, such as interesting old brooches, earrings or charms or new glass nuggets and chandelier prisms
Sewing needle and thread

For a completely natural look, alternative materials could include jute hessian to wrap around bundles of candles; jute string and an assortment of natural materials, such as shells, stones, seed heads, dried rosebuds and larch cones.

1. Bundle the candles together using a rubber band, which will be hidden under the decoration.

2. There are various ways in which you can now decorate your bundles of candles. You could simply tie a length of luxurious ribbon around the candles and tie it in an attractive bow. Velvets, silks or other slippery fabrics can be knotted in place or wrapped around the bundle and hot glued in place. Tuck under or glue the raw ends and conceal them with a few appropriately placed glass nuggets stuck in place. You could even sew a chandelier prism or pin an old brooch to the fabric or ribbon – the possibilities are endless.

3. Alternatively, wrap corrugated card around the bundle of candles. Hot glue in place and tie a ribbon around it in a frothy bow. Glue a few attractively marked shells on top.

VELVET BOOKMARKS

You will need

12in (30cm) length of wire-edged velvet ribbon
Fabric or craft glue
Sewing needle
Gold metallic embroidery thread
Charms, glass beads, star-shaped or round sequins

1. To make the pointed ends of the bookmark, fold the ribbon in half lengthways, right sides together, and hold it down. At each short end of the ribbon fold back the corners evenly, wrong sides together, to meet at the central fold. Glue down firmly.

2. Apply the glue all over the surface of the wrong side of the ribbon. Fold the length of ribbon in half accurately, matching the two pointed ends together and checking the edges. Press together and leave under a heavy book for about 1 hour until dry.

3. Using the needle and gold thread, stitch the pointed ends of the bookmark together, at the same time attaching a charm or glass bead to the point. Sew or glue other small flat charms to the bookmark, such as the star-shaped sequins shown here, if liked.

GLITTERING GOLD
CRACKER GIFT

You will need

Craft knife
Cardboard tubes from
*   2 toilet rolls*
15 x 7in (38 x 18cm) rectangle
*   of gold wrapping paper*
Tape measure
Pencil
Hot glue gun and glue stick,
*   or tube glue*
Small gift for cracker
Adhesive tape
Short length of colourful wide
*   sari braid*
Long glass-headed pin
Scissors
Narrow ribbon
Pinking shears

1. Cut one of the cardboard toilet roll tubes in half to make two shorter tubes.

2. Lay the gold paper in front of you, wrong side uppermost. Using a tape measure and pencil, find and mark the centre of one long side of the paper rectangle.

3. Lay the longest length of cardboard tube on the paper, against this long edge, and centre it over the pencil mark on the paper. Next, pencil a mark on the paper at either end of the cardboard tube. Then measure 2in (5cm) away from the marks, in the direction of the short sides of the rectangle of gold paper, and make more pencil marks – the space between these marks represents the gap between the tubes where the cracker will be pinched in and tied.

4. Align the shorter tubes against the last marks and make another mark at the end of each.

5. With the marked long side of the paper nearest you, run a line of glue along the very edge of the wrong side of the gold paper, where the single large tube will be, and roll the tube on to the glue. Repeat the process for the two smaller tubes, remembering to leave the marked gaps clear. Hold in place for a short while until the glue begins to adhere.

6. Roll up the cracker. If the gift to be enclosed is quite fat, insert it into the central tube before rolling up the cracker. If the item is small, it can be dropped in from one end afterwards.

7. Secure the cracker with a tiny piece of adhesive tape. Wrap the sari braid around the cracker and hold it in place with a pin.

8. Cut the narrow ribbon into two lengths. Tie one length around one end of the cracker in the gap between the lengths of tube. Pull fairly tightly to get the cracker shape, tie the ribbon into a bow and trim the ends with scissors. Drop your small gift in the open end of the cracker if you haven't already done so, before sealing it with the second length of ribbon tied in a bow.

9. Turn in the raw edges at each end of the sari braid and glue down. Replace the pin to hold the braid in position until the glue dries. If necessary adjust the ends of the cracker to ensure they are even. Trim the ends with pinking shears for a decorative finish.

Vibrant stamped & painted giftwrap

Rather than buy run-of-the-mill wrapping paper, why not have fun making your own? Create a few simple designs on brightly coloured paper. It is quick to do, and the materials are inexpensive and easy to find.

   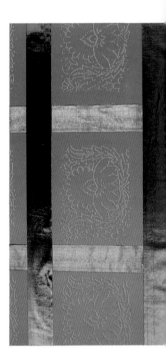

You will need

Sheets of coloured craft paper
Wide-tipped gold and silver
*   calligraphy pens*
Glitter glue pens in various colours
Rubber stamp
Matt emulsion paint in colours
*   of your choice*
Small paintbrush
Ribbon
Scissors
Craft glue

Large sheets of craft paper in practically every colour imaginable are available from art shops and specialist art material suppliers, as well as larger craft suppliers. The paper is graded into different thicknesses; the lighter or medium weight papers are best for wrapping presents. The very thick paper is too difficult to wrap or fold around a parcel, and will tear; it is also more expensive.

The possibilities for decorating the papers to create your own giftwrap are endless. You may already have one or two rubber stamps or a suitable stencil you could use. The simplest designs look the most stunning, especially in glitter glue, which comes in all the jewel colours. Steer clear of the really cheap glitter glues since their glitter content is minimal and the effect is lost. Choose a densely coloured

one – they usually come in clear plastic containers or "pens" and it is easy to see whether the glitter is densely packed or sparse.

Decide which colours look best together; the silver on vibrant turquoise looks fantastic, while the Indian blocked design of jade green on bright pink is a knockout – the two colours together look fluorescent. If you prefer pastel shades or neutrals, try bronze or gold on cream, raw

linen and parchment-coloured papers instead, for an easily achieved result, which actually looks very chic and expensive.

If the sheet of paper is for a specific gift, do stop to consider the size of the parcel and where the major part of the design should be – it would be a pity to lose it in the folded-in ends!

1. Start by laying the sheets of craft paper flat on a work surface where they can be left undisturbed to dry when you have finished.

2. For the first two papers pictured far left, draw a leaf pattern (or any freehand design – circles, squiggles and star shapes all look great) using a wide-tipped gold or silver calligraphy pen. Then outline the design with glitter glue in the same colour, linking the shapes. The glitter glue takes a while to dry, so do take great care not to smudge it.

3. Another option on a dark-coloured paper is to draw wavy ribbons – some solid, some patterned like ladders – using gold and silver calligraphy pens (see third picture opposite). Outline the "ribbons" as before with the relevant coloured glitter glue.

4. Lastly, to create an effect similar to the vibrant pink paper pictured, stamp the paper all over with an old Indian printing block covered in a brightly coloured matt emulsion paint. Once the paint is dry, cut a similarly coloured ribbon into lengths and stick it on the paper using a suitable craft glue.

Sari braid treasure bags

Vibrant Indian silk sari braids, intricately woven with rich gold and silver metallic threads come in a huge variety of colours and are perfect for making these treasure bags. Enclose a small gift and hang them on the tree – they make eye-catching decorations and exciting gifts to open on Christmas morning!

You will need

Scissors
4½–6in (11–15cm) wide sari braid
Tape measure
Long glass-headed pins
Sewing machine or needle and thread
Silk cord and small decorative tassels, or ribbon

Available by mail order and incredibly inexpensive, sari braids are suitably wide simply to fold in half into a bag shape and stitch together in a matter of minutes. Use silk cord and beaded tassels to draw up the tops, or ribbon threaded through. Enclose a small bottle of beautiful perfume, deliciously scented soaps, handmade chocolates or miniature bottles of favourite liqueurs.

1. Cut a length of sari braid approximately 15in (38cm) long. Turn under the two raw ends of the braid twice to make a double hem to avoid further fraying. Pin then machine or hand stitch the hems in place.

2. Fold the length of braid in half, right sides together, and pin the side seams. Machine or hand stitch, leaving small gaps in the side seams near the top of the bag if you wish to thread through a length of cord or ribbon for closing the bag (see picture, page 23).

3. Turn the stitched rectangle of fabric the right side out. If you are intending to use silk cord simply tied around the bag, cut the silk cord to length and stitch a small decorative tassel to each end. Tie the tasselled silk cord around the bag, near the top, and knot it loosely, or use a length of attractive ribbon and tie the loose ends in a bow.

If you have chosen to leave gaps in the side seam, thread your cord or ribbon through the casing formed at the top of the bag and only sew the decorative tassels on once the cord or ribbon is in place.

Two-hour transformations

Crackers and cards, rosebuds and lilies, beads and boxes – just some of the themes of this chapter. Combine ordinary household materials with more specialist items, such as sugar paste, abalone shells, decorative stones and dried rosebuds, into elegant crackers, a delicate necklace, handmade greetings cards, exquisite tree decorations and decorated boxes. Plenty of inspiration here to keep you occupied in the run-up to Christmas!

Manila crackers

It is hard to imagine these elegant crackers have been made from ordinary household materials – brown paper, white tissue and string. The tiny larch cones with their bronze metallic finish add a warm glow to the Christmas table.

You will need (per cracker)

Scissors
14 x 7in (35 x 18cm) rectangle of brown manila paper
15 x 14in (38 x 35cm) rectangle of white tissue paper
Tape measure
Hot glue gun and glue stick
Pencil
Length of cardboard tube from kitchen paper roll or similar, the diameter approx. 1¾–2in (4.5–5cm), cut into one 5¼in (13cm) length and two 2in (5cm) lengths
Jute string
Small gifts or cracker novelties
Small paintbrush
5 larch cones and 1–2 small pressed dried leaves
Acrylic bronze metallic paint
Disposable face mask
Bronze metallic powder

Larch cones are easy to find all year round. The spindly branches fall to the ground with the little cones still attached, and become part of the woodland carpet. Avoid blackened cones or any that are wet. If you find a larch wood, there will be plenty still on the trees, but I am always fortunate enough to find them on the ground during the summer and autumn.

Sheets of good-quality brown manila paper are often cheapest bought from a post office, local stationer's or newsagent's. Once it comes under the heading of "craft paper" the price goes up and the quality down.

1. Using scissors, cut the short sides of the brown paper rectangle in a decorative zigzag pattern.

2. Fold the white tissue paper in half to give a double thickness of tissue, measuring 15 x 7in (38 x 18cm). Make a "fringe" at both short sides of the folded tissue rectangle by making a series of parallel cuts about 1in (2.5cm) deep, close together.

3. Lay the folded white tissue on top of the brown paper, overlapping it slightly at each end. Hot glue along the long edges of the brown paper and stick the tissue paper down.

4. With the tissue paper still uppermost, and using a tape measure and pencil, find and mark the centre of one long side of the paper rectangle.

5. Lay the longest cardboard tube on the tissue paper, against this long side, and centre it over the mark on the paper. Now mark

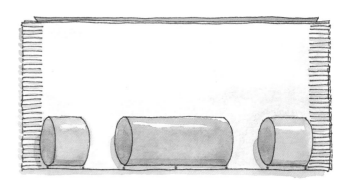

the paper at either end of the tube. Measure 2in (5cm) away from the marks, towards the decorated edges of the paper, and make more pencil marks – the space between these marks represents the gap between the tubes where the cracker will be pinched in and tied.

6. Align the small 2in (5cm) tubes against the last marks and make another mark at the end of each.

7. With the marked long edge of the paper nearest you, hot glue a line on the very edge of the paper between the marks where the centre tube will be, and roll the tube on to the glue. Repeat the process for the two smaller tubes, remembering to leave the gaps.

8. Roll the cracker up firmly. Hot glue along the length of the edge of paper and hold it firmly in position until the glue adheres.

9. Cut two lengths of jute string. Tie one length around one end of the cracker in the gap between the lengths of tube. Pull tight, tie into a bow and trim the ends with scissors.

10. Drop any small gifts or cracker novelties in the other end of the cracker, before tying the second length of string in a bow. If the ends of the cracker look a little unbalanced, adjust them now by cutting.

11. Using a small paintbrush, paint the small larch cones and leaves with acrylic bronze metallic paint. Leave until almost dry. Wearing a disposable face mask since it is dangerous to inhale the powder, gingerly shake the tiniest amount of bronze metallic powder on to the cones and leaves. Once they are dry, carefully hot glue into place on the crackers.

Rosebud necklace

This exquisitely delicate rosebud and bead necklace is very feminine and pretty, and surprisingly simple to make. Make two and use one to embellish a special gift.

You will need

Scissors
Beading needle and white beading thread
Seed beads and bugle beads in amethyst, fuchsia pink and green
Tiny pearls
Packet of dried rosebuds
Small wooden chopping board
Large sewing needle

1. Cut a length of beading thread long enough make a loop to fit comfortably over someone's head. Thread the beading needle with the thread, then pass it through the first seed bead. Tie the thread around the bead to form a knot.

2. Continue to thread beads on to the thread, choosing different coloured seed and bugle beads and tiny pearls, until you have a 2½in (6.5cm) length of beads.

3. Tip a few dried rosebuds on to a chopping board. Using a large sewing needle, pierce a hole through the green part of each rosebud, at the top of the stem beneath the flower head.

4. Thread a rosebud on to the beaded string, then follow with another 2½in (6.5cm) section of seed, bugle and pearl beads. Continue the process, ensuring

the dried rosebuds are placed at equal distances with the beads in between.

5. When you have filled the length of beading thread with beads and rosebuds, secure the final bead with a knot as before. Knot the two loose ends together firmly to make a necklace.

EMBELLISHING A GIFT

Make a second string of beads and rosebuds in the same way. Secure the ends but do not tie them together. Instead, use the delicate string to decorate a gift.

First wrap the gift in white crêpe paper and secure the ends with adhesive tape. Then wrap the white crêpe parcel in a piece

of rainbow cellophane and secure the ends discreetly. Carefully tie the string of beaded rosebuds

around the gift for an unusual and unique finish and secure the two ends with a knot.

Unusual greetings cards

Handmade cards are a joy to receive and you could easily expand upon the ideas given here. Develop an "eye" for the potential use of remnants of ribbon and fabric, an old cake frill, a few sequins or beads, shells and pretty stones or a broken necklace, and you will become expert in making your own cards.

Hot glue gun and glue stick, or a clear or opaque glue suitable for sticking fabric and paper, plus brush
Scraps of metallic red crêpe paper
Gold relief outliner (contour paste)
Gold braid

It is always fun creating something from nothing, especially when the materials are already to hand, with the exception perhaps of the sheet of gold card. These simple ideas are in the traditional colours of red, green and gold, but once you get started, you are sure to come up with your own inspired designs!

Before deciding on the size of greetings cards you wish to make, it is a good idea to source some envelopes first.

1. Turn the sheet of gold card face down. Using a tape measure or ruler and a pencil, measure and mark a line down the centre of the card lengthways. Place a straight edge or metal ruler on the line and use it as a guide against which to lightly run a craft knife in order to score the card. This enables the card to be folded more easily. Cut across the card to make two or three greetings cards of a size to fit your envelopes. Fold the cards in half along the scored fold line.

2. For the large gold card pictured, cut a rectangle of green velvet, larger than one of your best dried leaves. Glue it on to the front of the card, leaving a margin all round of about 1–1½in (2.5–4cm). Stick your chosen leaf on to the velvet and press flat until it adheres to the fabric.

3. To create a "frame" for the velvet, cut the metallic red crêpe paper into four strips to the necessary length, and about 1in (2.5cm) wide. Cut a zigzag design on the inside edges of the strips. On the two longer strips intended for the vertical sides of the frame, cut out a triangle at each end on the outside edge of the strips. Glue all four strips into position on the card.

SNAZZY SCRAP CARDS

You will need

Sheets of A4 gold card
Tape measure and straight edge, or metal ruler
Pencil
Craft knife and scissors
Remnants of green velvet
Pressed dried leaves, sprayed gold or silver (see page 16) and decorated with added metal flakes (optional)

4. Use the gold relief outliner around the very edge of the velvet rectangle to outline the velvet and stop it from fraying. Next draw a continuous line with the gold outliner around the outside of the red crepe paper frame. Highlight the zigzags with a similar pattern in gold.

SMALL GOLD CARD

A variation on the above design is to stick the green velvet on to the gold card and mount a smaller rectangle of red crepe paper on top of it. Glue a decorated oak leaf on the red paper and outline both the crepe paper and the velvet with the gold contour pen. Finally, stick a remnant of gold braid around the edge of the velvet to form a frame.

COLLAGE ON RED CARD

To make the red card illustrated on the previous page, which is 4½ x 6in (11 x 15cm), use small sharp scissors to cut wavy, slightly scalloped edges freehand. Stick a rectangular shape of torn gold and white script paper on the card. On top of this stick a square of blue foil sweet paper and gold foil chocolate paper cut into odd wavy shapes. Use two pressed dried hazel leaves, a tissue paper butterfly and two flat-backed acrylic "jewels" surrounded by gold wire thread to complete the collage.

LEAF DESIGN CARDS

You will need

Tape measure and straight edge, or metal ruler
Fine pencil
1 sheet of handmade paper
Artist's acrylic tube paint in yellow ochre or raw sienna, Venetian red or red oxide
"Palette"
Rubber leaf stamp (see below)
Small artist's paintbrush
Gold glitter glue (pen or applicator)
Sequins
Hot glue gun and glue stick
Small colourful pressed dried leaves
Small scissors
Gold foil cake frill or ribbon
Brown manila paper
Paper edge-cutters (optional)
Can of florist's silver, gold or bronze metallic spray paint, or acrylic bronze or pewter metallic paint, bronze or silver metallic powder and disposable face mask

Instead of a leaf stamp you could use pressed dried leaves to create leafy designs. Paint the leaves on their undersides with acrylic tube paint in your chosen colour, then press them firmly on the paper to leave an imprint (see Pewter Painted Leaf Paper, page 16).

As before, you need to know the size of your envelopes before you make a start.

1. Measure the size of cards required to fit the envelopes and draw fine pencil lines to mark out the handmade paper accordingly. Hold the ruler or straight edge firmly on the pencil lines, and carefully tear the paper along it. Fold into a card shape.

2. Squeeze a little of your chosen artist's acrylic tube paint on to a "palette" and apply it sparingly to the rubber stamp using a small paintbrush. Stamp leaves at random on to the hand-made paper for the background design and leave to dry.

3. The options now are endless. You could apply gold glitter glue

to mark the central vein of the stamped leaves. If you want to add a few sequins, apply a tiny amount of hot glue to the paper and place the sequins on top, taking great care not to burn your fingers. Alternatively, you could glue pressed dried leaves on top of the painted leafy background pattern.

4. To finish your cards, you could cut out a narrow strip of decorative cake frill and stick it to the underside of the front opening edge of each card, or add a ribbon bow to the front.

5. Alternatively, cut a rectangle of manila paper ¾in (2cm) larger than your whole decorated card. Fold it in half and cut frilly edges using sharp scissors or edge-cutters. Slip inside the card to

check the fit and adjust it if necessary. This insert could be sprayed with florist's silver, gold or bronze metallic spray paint. Alternatively, paint the paper with acrylic bronze or pewter metallic paint, on to which a small amount of bronze or silver metallic powder is shaken and knocked off again for a glittering effect. Do wear a disposable face mask when using metallic powders as it is dangerous to inhale them. Glue the insert to the inside spine of the card.

6. Torn music sheet, shells and pressed dried leaves painted with acrylic bronze metallic paint are other possible decorative options but you are bound to have other ideas of your own.

PAINTED CARDS IN PURPLES & PINKS

You will need

*Thick art paper in purple,
    pink and white, or white
    handmade or cartridge
    paper and coloured
    craft papers*
Ruler and pencil
Sharp scissors
Stiff card
*Low-contact masking tape
    (optional)*
Small artist's paintbrush
*Artist's acrylic tube paint in
    deep violet*
Ribbon or string
*Sheesha mirror glass (see page
    110) or assorted sequins*
*Craft glue or hot glue gun
    and glue stick*
Lining brush
*Scraps of tissue paper or tissue
    paper cut-outs*
*Artist's concentrated liquid
    colour in interference
    (opalescent) medium
    magenta*
Clear cellophane
*Silver glitter glue or silver
    wide-tipped calligraphy
    pen*

It can be great fun experimenting with designs, colours and materials for Christmas cards and gift tags. Not only that, your creations will be unique! These cards were inspired by the lilac colours of pot-pourri. Paint simple patterns using thinned acrylic tube paints and opalescent paints on to white handmade paper, or white tissue paper. Here are just a few ideas to inspire – you may wish to use a different range of colours and decorations.

This is a great project for family participation – the cards are such fun to make and my grandchildren love "helping" with the preparation work! If, like me, you have a lengthy Christmas card list, you will need to produce masses of cards. Organize your table top or work surface into a conveyor belt system first. Have piles of ready-cut folded blank cards in various colours, graded into sizes. As before, the availability of envelopes will tend to dictate the size of the cards, so check this first. Have ready another pile of white handmade paper squares or rectangles, which have been torn against the straight edge of a ruler for a lovely natural effect. You will need a few handmade stencils; scraps of tissue paper, which can be pleated, or any pretty tissue designs cut from wrapping papers – such as the butterfly and flowers used here; and cellophane squares or rectangles to overwrap the cards. Have handy small containers of sequins, tin shapes or sheesha mirror glass, as well as lengths of ribbon or string – a good way of using up last year's giftwrap and trimmings.

1. Decide on the paper for your cards and determine the size according to your envelopes. Using a ruler and pencil, mark out the cards accordingly. Cut out the cards with scissors or, for a natural look – especially suitable with handmade paper, hold the ruler firmly on the pencil lines, and carefully tear the paper along it. Fold into card shapes.

2. To make a simple stencil, draw your chosen shape, such as a star or a snowflake, on to a piece of stiff card – the card from a cereal box would be suitable. Cut out the shape.

3. Place the stencil over the front of a blank card, ensuring that it is centred. Secure at the corners with masking tape, if liked, or hold it firm and flat with your hand, while painting in your chosen colour. Decorate with ribbon and sheesha mirror glass or sequins glued in place.

4. The layered cards are a matter of making it up as you go along to build a pretty picture. Layers add to the effect and it is simple to mount white paper on to a darker thick paper, like the purple shown here. Look, too, for papers and objects in the same colour which can be used, or add a bow or tassel for extra effect.

5. For the stripy, layered cards, first paint vertical stripes on the white paper, using a lining brush, which makes it much easier to achieve straight lines. When the paint is dry, glue pleated scraps of tissue paper and/or tissue cut-outs and a few sequins or tin shapes on top, and attach short lengths of ribbon.

6. Another option is to use a simple design of opalescent liquid paint on good-quality art paper. Overlaying the card with a piece of clear cellophane reflects the pearly quality of the paint in a magical way and makes an attractive card. Other decorative possibilities include using silver glitter-glue or a wide-tipped silver calligraphy pen – go ahead and experiment!

Icing sugar lilies

These lilies look exquisite and very unusual although they are simple to make. You can take the project further by mounting the finished lilies on to wire stems covered with green florist's tape, or perhaps be even more adventurous and use them to make a central table decoration or candle sconce.

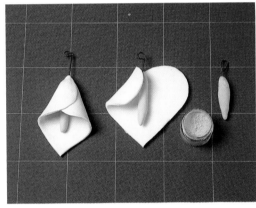
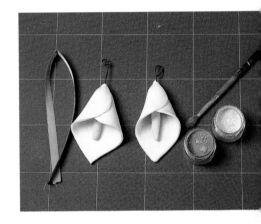

You will need

Vegetable fat
Cutting board
7oz (200g) packet of white sugar paste
Rolling pin
Cutting wheel or sharp knife
Edible food colouring powder in yellow, green and silver
Florist's wire
Narrow pretty ribbon
Small artist's paintbrush

White sugar paste is available from professional cake suppliers or large craft suppliers. It comes already moist in a vacuum-sealed pack and can be kept in the refrigerator. This quantity is sufficient to make six flowers.

1. Rub a little vegetable fat on to the cutting board to create a lightly greased surface.

2. Take one-sixth of the sugar paste and mould it in your hands until soft and pliable. Pat into a rough circle, place on the cutting board and roll out to a thickness of approximately 1/10in (2.5mm).

3. Using a cutting wheel or sharp knife, cut out a heart shape measuring 3 1/2 x 3 1/2in (9 x 9cm). (Use a paper template if it helps.)

4. Take a little of the remaining paste, roll it into a ball and add a little yellow food colouring powder. Keep moulding and rolling until the colour is evenly dispersed throughout the paste.

Roll the yellow paste into a conical shape, about 2in (5cm) long, to form the yellow centre of the flower.

5. Cut a 3in (7.5cm) length of florist's wire. Push it about 1 1/2in (4cm) into the shaped yellow paste. Place the wired yellow centre on top of the heart shape in the "V", with the wire protruding from the top of the heart.

6. Fold one side of the paste heart down over the yellow flower centre, towards the middle of the heart. Moisten the top edge of the other side with water and fold over to overlap the first. Press down and hold together until the two sides have adhered to one another.

7. Bend the top of the protruding wire to make a loop. Thread with the ribbon and leave to dry for 2 hours before painting. Use the remaining paste to make five more lilies in the same way.

8. The lilies can be left white or painted with edible food colourings, as here, where a little dry green powder has been painted in the centre of each lily. The final touch is the fine dusting of iridescent silver powder over parts of the flowers.

9. Hang the lilies in a dry damp-free place. They will take 24 hours to dry out thoroughly. The lilies are best stored in an airtight jar if they are to be kept for any length of time.

Portrait giftboxes

These delightful little boxes are a pleasure to make and give. The box itself can be the present, or it can hold a small gift wrapped in tissue paper. Available from craft suppliers, the cardboard boxes are inexpensive and lightweight; they come in a variety of attractive shapes and sizes and are quick to paint. Here are a few ideas of how to decorate them in an old-fashioned style.

You will need

Small cardboard or plywood boxes
Small household paintbrush
Matt emulsion paint in mint green and putty pink
240 grade sandpaper
Portrait pictures cut from greetings cards or magazines or colourcopied images
Small scissors
Stick adhesive
Gold relief outliner (contour paste)
Braid, ribbon and gold foil cake frill

1. Take each box and paint it all over – the lid and the box itself, inside and out and underneath – with matt emulsion paint. Allow to dry thoroughly.

2. All boxes will require a second coat of paint. For boxes made of plywood, you will need to sand the surfaces gently between the coats of paint. Use fine sandpaper and work in the same direction as the grain. Remove the dust and apply a second coat of paint to all the surfaces. Leave to dry.

3. Try your chosen picture against each box lid to check that it fits accurately. Cut to size and glue in place.

4. If the portrait does not fit the size of the box lid exactly, use the gold relief outliner to draw scrolls, squiggles, a trellis effect or any other pattern around the portrait. The idea is to overlap the edge of the picture in the form of a "frame". Do take care not to touch the gold outliner as you continue to work, as it dries quite slowly. Leave for at least 1 hour to dry – test it by barely touching it with your finger to be sure it has hardened.

5. Cut a length of braid to edge the portrait if liked, and use braid, ribbon or gold foil cake frill cut down to a narrow size around the outside edge of the lid. Glue in place. Tie and glue a pretty ribbon around the middle of the box itself or draw more patterns using the gold relief outliner – the possibilities are endless and you can have fun experimenting.

RED & GOLD HEXAGONAL BOX

You will need

Hexagonal cardboard box, approx. 2½in (6.5cm) across
Jam jar with lid
Artist's acrylic tube paint in metallic red
Small paintbrush
Ruler or straight edge
Portrait picture cut from greetings card or magazine, or colour-copied image
Stick adhesive
Gold ribbon or braid
Gold glitter glue
Gold stars (optional)

1. Before you begin painting the box, fill the jam jar with water and squeeze a little metallic red acrylic tube paint on to the lid to use it as a palette. Dip your paintbrush in the water and, using a minimal amount of water, thin the paint on the palette slightly to a usable but not watery consistency.

2. Paint the box all over, both inside and out, with the metallic red paint. Allow to dry thoroughly. Apply a second coat and leave to dry.

3. Holding a ruler or straight edge firmly in place on your chosen picture, tear carefully around the edge of the picture to form a hexagonal shape that will fit on the box lid, leaving sufficient room around the edge of the box in which to draw an outline with glitter glue. Glue the picture on to the lid.

4. Cut a length of gold ribbon or braid to fit around the outside edge of the lid. Glue in place.

5. Outline the edge of the picture with glitter glue, and pick out something in the portrait to highlight, for example one or two curls of hair, as here.

6. Glue three stars, if using, on each hexagonal side panel and leave the box to dry.

43

Decorated abalone shells

These decorated shells are very appealing, and bring to mind Fabergé's eggs and fabulous jewellery. They make unusual gifts as trinket dishes of delicate beauty for use on the dressing table to hold earrings and other small items. They also make ideal receptacles for small scented guest soaps.

You will need

Large abalone shell
Sea shell or tiny abalone shell
Can of florist's silver metallic
 spray paint (optional)
Small frosted glass cherub
 (see supplier's list)
Two-part epoxy glue
Selection of decorative items such as
 glass nuggets, glass marbles,
 chandelier-style crystals,
 faceted beads, pearls, flat-
 backed acrylic or glass jewels
Scissors
String of pearl beads
Hot glue gun and glue stick
 (optional)

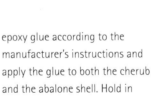
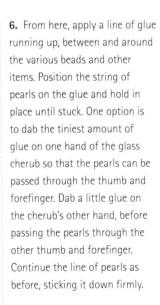

There are plenty of options for decorating large abalone shells. You will most easily find them in seaside shops selling shells, or possibly the larger craft suppliers.

You could use an old pearl necklace for this project. Once it is cut to the required lengths, use a spot of hot glue on each end to stop the last beads coming off the thread. An old necklace with knots in between the beads is ideal. If the beads are loose, however, take care that they don't come off the thread before you have a chance to glue the last bead in place!

1. Wash and dry the abalone shell thoroughly to ensure the surface is clean and grease- and dust-free.

2. If you wish to spray the sea shell, shake the can of spray paint well for a couple of minutes before use. Working in a well-ventilated area, spray the shell silver and leave to dry.

3. Decide on the exact position of the glass cherub – probably on the widest part of the edge of the abalone shell. Prepare the epoxy glue according to the manufacturer's instructions and apply the glue to both the cherub and the abalone shell. Hold in place until the glue hardens.

4. Decide on the positions of the silver-sprayed or tiny abalone shell and the various glass and acrylic decorative items you have chosen to use. Glue them in place, one by one, holding each until it is firmly stuck.

5. Cut two lengths of pearls approximately 5–7in (12.5–18cm). Secure the beads at each end if necessary (see above). Dab epoxy glue behind the silver-sprayed or tiny abalone shell and hold one end of the string of pearls on it for a few seconds until secure.

6. From here, apply a line of glue running up, between and around the various beads and other items. Position the string of pearls on the glue and hold in place until stuck. One option is to dab the tiniest amount of glue on one hand of the glass cherub so that the pearls can be passed through the thumb and forefinger. Dab a little glue on the cherub's other hand, before passing the pearls through the other thumb and forefinger. Continue the line of pearls as before, sticking it down firmly.

7. Thread the other length of pearls in a similar fashion around the edge of the shell in the opposite direction. Glue firmly in place.

Beaded velvet frames & boxes

Picture frames and jewellery boxes covered in richly coloured velvets are available ready-made from some suppliers and are ripe for decoration. They make colourful Christmas gifts, embellished with beads, glass nuggets and glass or acrylic decorative stones, caught with a few stitches or glued in place.

RED RECTANGULAR VELVET FRAME

You will need

Red velvet-covered rectangular picture frame
Beading needle and beading thread
Seed beads: 8 midnight blue, 8 pink and 2 gold
Faceted flat-backed "jewels" with 2 holes for sewing on: 4 blue stars, 4 pink ovals and 1 gold moon
Two-part epoxy glue
Jewellery pliers
Smooth flat-backed "jewels" for gluing: 2 blue round, 2 pink tear-shaped and 1 green round
Two 4in (10cm) lengths of thick gold thread
Sewing needle and thin gold thread

Good craft suppliers, or specifically bead suppliers, stock a vast range of beads, faceted and smooth acrylic or glass flat-backed "jewels" (decorative stones), rhinestone crystals, sequins and spangles, as well as coloured glass nuggets. Some have holes for sewing on, others are for use with glue.

A beading needle is necessary because this is the only needle fine enough to pass through a tiny seed bead. It is also longer than an ordinary sewing needle. Beading thread is used because it is much finer and stronger than ordinary thread, which could be cut by sharp-edged beads. Buy beading needles and thread from bead or general craft suppliers and good needlework shops.

1. Begin by stitching the decorations in each corner of the frame. Thread the beading needle with beading thread and tie a knot at the end. Make a small securing stitch in the velvet, which will be hidden out of sight beneath the blue star. Pass the threaded needle through a midnight blue seed bead then pass the needle back down into the velvet. Bring the needle back up, through a hole in the star, then again back into the velvet. Pass the needle beneath the velvet of the frame, underneath the star, and bring it up through the hole on the other side of the star. Pass the needle

down into the fabric, then up and through a second seed bead. Pass the needle down into the velvet for the last time, to hold the seed bead, then out to the edge of the frame. Make a small slip stitch where it cannot be seen to secure the thread; then snip.

2. Repeat this process at the other three corners of the frame, stitching a blue star with a blue seed bead on either side of it.

3. Prepare the epoxy glue according to the manufacturer's instructions. Using jewellery pliers to avoid getting glue on your hands, glue a blue round jewel in the middle of either side of the frame.

4. Glue a pink tear-shaped jewel in the middle of the top and the bottom edge of the frame.

5. Stitch a pink oval either side of the glued pink tear-shaped jewels, top and bottom of the frame, as you did for the blue star, this time using a pink seed bead at each end of the ovals.

6. Next, stitch the gold moon, with a gold seed bead on either side of it, above the pink tear-

shaped jewel on the top edge of the frame. Glue a green round jewel on the bottom edge.

7. Finally, wind a 4in (10cm) length of thick gold thread in a decorative spiral around one or both blue round jewels on the sides of the frame. Using an ordinary sewing needle and thin gold thread, secure the spiral in place with small neat stitches.

RED SQUARE FRAME

This is decorated in a similar fashion. Stitch a blue oval flat-backed jewel with three blue seed beads at each end of it in each corner of the frame. Stitch a pink round flat-backed jewel in the middle of each side of the frame with a pink seed bead either side.

Stitch a flat-backed gold moon above the pink jewel on the top edge of the frame, with a gold seed bead either side of it.

Using epoxy glue carefully as before, stick three tiny gold jewels above and to either side of the pink jewel on the bottom edge of the frame.

GREEN VELVET BOX

You will need

Two-part epoxy glue
1 dark green smooth, flat-backed large oval "jewel" for gluing
Green velvet-covered square box
Jewellery pliers
Faceted flat-backed tiny round "jewels" for gluing: 4 red, 3 gold and 2 pale green

Beading needle and fine gold thread
Faceted flat-backed oval "jewels" with 2 holes for sewing on: 4 pink and 2 pale green
Scissors
Gold braid

1. Prepare a little epoxy glue according to the manufacturer's instructions. Smear glue on the back of the large green oval jewel and stick it in the centre of the box lid, using jewellery pliers to avoid getting glue on your hands.

2. Similarly, apply glue to the tiny red jewels, positioning one in each corner of the box lid.

3. Using the beading needle and fine gold thread, sew a pink oval near each end of the central green oval, passing the needle beneath the velvet cover to then stitch the paler green ovals close to the sides of the central dark green oval. Sew the two remaining pink ovals in place – at a slight angle either side of one of the central pink ones.

4. To complete the top of the lid, glue the three gold and the two pale green tiny jewels in place as illustrated, using jewellery pliers as before.

5. Cut the gold braid to length and attach it around the box lid, using small neat stitches.

BLUE VELVET BOX

Simply glue coloured glass nuggets to the velvet surface of a round box and lid.

Three-hour thrills

For Christmassy surroundings place gilded candle pots on the table, or opt for a shimmering white look. Combine white handmade paper with coloured tissue paper to create delightful crackers that are too good to pull! Make sumptuous velvet Christmas stockings with leftover fabric; add a touch of genius and sparkle to packaging with tissue paper and cellophane; and fill bronzed urns with fresh greenery and fruit.

Candle pots

*Painted terracotta flowerpots make ideal containers for pillar or ordinary candles.
Small gilded pots add a warm glow to the Christmas celebrations, while white pearly
painted ones shimmer prettily with the addition of sequins, pearl beads, glass pebbles
or tiny white sea shells.*

GILDED POTS

You will need

*Terracotta flowerpots, 3½–4in
(9–10cm) tall
Can of florist's gold metallic
spray paint
Small paintbrush
Acrylic gold size
3-4 sheets of Dutch metal
transfer leaf
Soft brush
Block of dry oasis (dry florist's
foam), approx. 8 x 4 x 4in
(20 x 10 x 10cm)
Craft knife
Candles
Dried lichen or plant material such
as small fir cones, larch cones,
seed heads or nuts*

Dried lichen is available from
florist's or you could collect your
own from fallen branches while
out walking. If you want to use
fresh moss, flowers or foliage
around the base of the candles,
use wet oasis instead of dry oasis
and soak it in lukewarm water for
about 5 minutes, before cutting it
to fit the pots. Keep the wet oasis
damp and spray the fresh plants
to keep them looking alive. If they
wilt, remove them and place in a
bowl of fresh water at room
temperature until they revive!

There follow two simple ways
of covering terracotta pots in
gold – the choice is yours. If
possible try to find the lovely old
pots with straight sides (long
Toms) as they have rougher, more
interesting surfaces.

1. If the flowerpots are old,
scrub them clean and leave to
dry out well, remembering that
terracotta is porous.

2. Take the can of gold spray
paint and shake it well for a
couple of minutes before
beginning – remember to keep
shaking it in between spraying.
Working in a well-ventilated area,
spray the flowerpots with gold
paint and leave them to dry.

3. First decide on the pattern
you would like gilded on your
pots. It could be squares, spots,
stripes, a bow or all over.

4. Using a small paintbrush,
brush the acrylic gold size on to
the gold-sprayed flowerpots in

your chosen pattern. Leave for
at least 15 minutes until the gold
size is tacky.

5. Take a sheet of Dutch metal
transfer leaf and gently press it
on to the gold-sized areas,
smoothing your fingers over the
sheet until all of the leaf has
transferred to the surface of the
pots. Remove the backing tissue.
Continue until your design is
completely gilded.

6. Go over the sprayed and
gilded pots gently with a soft
brush to remove any excess
Dutch metal leaf.

7. Cut the oasis into pieces to
fit inside the pots, using a craft
knife. Place a candle in each pot,

add the oasis and pack it tightly around each candle to keep it firmly in place.

8. If using dry oasis to pack around the base of each candle, conceal it by covering it loosely with dried lichen or other plant material, gilded if liked.

9. Alternatively, if using soaked pieces of wet oasis to hold the candles in the pots, cover the oasis with fresh moss, flowers or foliage. Keep the oasis damp and spray the fresh plants to stop them wilting.

ALTERNATIVE "GILDING" METHOD

Another way of decorating the flowerpots is to use gilding cream (see picture, page 50). This is available from craft shops or art suppliers, and comes in small pots in several colours of gold, ranging from pale gold to a deep

rich antique colour. You will also need a small quantity of white spirit in a glass jam jar and a small paintbrush.

1. Prepare your flowerpots as before. Then, for the first coat, dip your paintbrush into a little white spirit before dipping it into the gilding cream. The white spirit will thin the gilt cream slightly, allowing you to brush the cream on to the pots in the same way as paint. Leave to dry.

2. For the second coat apply the cream neat from the pot.

3. Leave to dry completely, before buffing with a soft cloth for a shiny finish; otherwise leave as it is for a matt finish.

4. Complete the pots with oasis, candles and foliage or plant material as before.

PEARLY WHITE POTS

You will need

Terracotta flowerpots, 3½-4in (9-10cm) tall
Matt emulsion paint in white
Small household paintbrush
Artist's concentrated liquid colour in iridescent white
Small paintbrush
Hot glue gun and glue stick or two-part epoxy glue
Pearl beads or a broken necklace
Silver heart-shaped sequins
Pillar candles
Craft knife
Block of dry oasis (dry florist's foam), approx. 8 x 4 x 4in (20 x 10 x 10cm)
Glass nuggets or tiny white sea shells

1. Prepare your terracotta flowerpots as before.

2. Paint the flowerpots all over with the white emulsion paint

and leave to dry. Apply a second and third coat if necessary, allowing the paint to dry completely between coats.

3. Complete the painting with a coat of the pearly white paint to give a shimmering delicate effect. Leave to dry.

4. Using hot or epoxy glue (the latter prepared according to the manufacturer's instructions), stick pearl beads and heart-shaped sequins around the rims of the pots to decorate. Leave the glue to dry well.

5. Place a pillar candle in the centre of each pot. Cut the dry oasis into pieces, as before, and pack tightly around the candles to keep them firmly in place.

6. Scatter loose glass nuggets or tiny white sea shells around the base of the candles to cover the dry oasis.

White velvet giftbox

Snowy white velvet adds a luxuriously seasonal touch and totally transforms a simple wooden box with a loose lid. The box is a useful size, suitable for storing art materials, sewing kit, letters and stationery, or to display in a bedroom. Wire-edged sheer ribbon twisted into a rose is the final decorative touch.

You will need

Small lidded wooden box
White velvet or Dralon
Tape measure
Scissors
Pencil or ballpoint pen
Hot glue gun and glue stick or fabric glue
Gold foil cake frill or roll of decorative foil (available from a professional cake icing supplier)
Gold card
Gold wide sari braid
Long glass-headed lampshade or dressmaking pins
White, wide wire-edged sheer ribbon
Gold foil leaf-shaped cake decoration

1. To calculate the quantity of velvet required to cover your box, measure the depth of the box and add sufficient to allow for turning under the raw edges of the fabric at the top and bottom – a good ½in (1.5cm) per raw edge. Measure all around the sides of the box to give the total length of fabric required to cover the sides of the box, again allowing a little extra for turning under the raw edges.

2. To measure the velvet required to cover the base of the box, place the fabric wrong side uppermost and stand the box on top. Using a pencil or ballpoint pen, mark the base of the box on the fabric. Cut a good ½in (1.5cm) outside the marked shape to allow for the raw edges as before.

3. The last calculation is to determine the velvet required for the lid of the box. Measure the dimensions of the top of the lid, add sufficient for the depth of the lid, i.e. the sides of the lid, and allow an extra ½in (1.5cm), as before, for the raw edges.

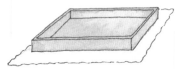

4. Having cut the velvet to the necessary measurements, start with the long strip of velvet for the sides of the box. Turn under the ½in (1.5cm) of fabric allowed for the raw edges along one long edge and the two short edges of the strip of fabric.

5. Apply hot glue to the sides of the box. Aligning the long turned edge of the velvet strip with the top edges of the box, stick the fabric to the sides of the box, carefully smoothing it into place and allowing the raw edge to overhang the bottom of the box.

6. Turn the box upside down and fold over the raw edge hanging over the base of the box all round. Glue it in place, turning the fabric neatly at the corners. If necessary, snip the fabric at the corners if it becomes too bulky.

7. Take the piece of fabric for the base of the box. Turn under and glue all four raw edges to neaten the piece of velvet, then glue it to the base of the box, over the stuck-down raw edges of the glued side strip, for a neat finish.

8. Turn under and glue all four raw edges on the piece of velvet for the lid of the box. Cut the gold foil cake frill into four lengths to match the outside

edges of the neatened piece of velvet, and to a width to match the depth of the lid plus an additional ¾in (2cm) to allow the scalloped edge to protrude decoratively beneath the velvet.

9. Place the neatened piece of velvet wrong side uppermost. With the wrong side of the cake frill also facing uppermost, stick a strip in place along one edge of the velvet to cover the glued turned edges and protrude by the ¾in (2cm) allowed for. Repeat with the remaining three strips, overlapping the frill and sticking it down at each corner.

10. Cut the gold card into a square or rectangle, as appropriate for your box, to cover both the velvet and the cake

decoration, trimming it back slightly to expose the scalloped edge of the cake frill. With the wrong side of the velvet and cake decoration still uppermost, lay the card on top with the gold side uppermost and glue in place. All three layers should now be well stuck together.

11. Apply glue to the top of the box lid, turn it upside down and place it in the middle of the gold card. Press down firmly. Apply

more glue to the sides of the box lid and bend and stick the card to the lid sides, pressing firmly and pinching the card together at the corners to give the pagoda look.

12. Cut a length of gold sari braid to wrap around the box, allowing a little extra for turning under the raw edges. Attach the braid to the box in a couple of

places, using only a small amount of glue and holding it in place on the velvet with glass-headed pins until the glue adheres.

13. To finish the box, twist a length of wire-edged sheer ribbon into a rose shape (see page 14) and glue it on to the box lid, together with a leaf-shaped cake decoration.

Rosebud & pot-pourri crackers

These crackers are not made to pull apart since they are far too lovely to tear up. They are more suitable as a way of presenting a special small gift. Instead of wrapping it in a giftbox, it is in the cracker and can be removed by untying one end.

You will need (per cracker)

Tape measure or ruler
Small scissors
2 sheets of vibrant pink and deep purple tissue paper
2 sheets of handmade white paper
Hot glue gun and glue stick
Pencil
Length of cardboard tube from kitchen paper roll or similar, the diameter approx. 1¾in (4.5cm), cut into one 4in (10cm) length and two 1¾in (4.5cm) lengths
Purple narrow braid or ribbon
Natural deep pink or crimson small dried roses and dried rose petals

A sheet of handmade paper inspired this project. If, like me, you grow roses and herbs and make your own pot-pourri, this is an ideal project with almost all "free" ingredients! Otherwise you can buy the most beautiful dried rosebuds and petals from good herbalists, but do try to avoid the over-poweringly perfumed ones, which are extremely unnatural.

1. Measure and cut out a double layer (2 sheets) of pink tissue paper 8¾ x 15in (22 x 38cm), and a double layer (2 sheets) of purple tissue paper 8¾ x 14in (22 x 35cm).

2. Measure and cut out a piece of handmade paper 8 x 12½in (20 x 31cm).

3. Fold the purple layers of tissue in half lengthways. Use sharp scissors to cut a scalloped edge along the two short sides of the rectangle then open the tissue paper out again and cut a scalloped edge along one long side of the rectangle. Similarly, cut a scalloped edge along one long side only of the pink tissue in the same way.

4. Lay the handmade white paper, wrong side uppermost, on the work surface. Lay the purple sheets of tissue paper on top, aligning the long unscalloped edge with one of the long edges of the handmade paper and ensuring the tissue overlaps the handmade paper equally at each end of the cracker.

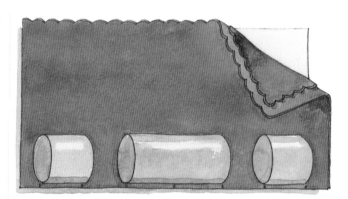

5. Run a fine line of hot glue along the long edge of the handmade paper, and gently press the long unscalloped edge of purple tissue on to it. Add a couple of tiny blobs, or a very short fine line of glue on the edge of the purple to keep the sheets of tissue together.

6. Lay the double thickness of pink tissue on top of the purple, aligning it against the long glued edge and overlapping the other papers equally at the ends of the cracker, where the pink paper will protrude further than the others. Run a small amount of glue along the unscalloped long edge of the pink paper and gently press down on to the purple tissue. Add a couple of tiny blobs between the long unscalloped edges of the pink to keep the sheets of tissue together in the same way as before.

7. Using a tape measure or ruler and pencil, find and mark the centre of the long unscalloped side of the pink rectangle that you have glued. Lay the longest length of cardboard tube on the tissue paper, against this long side, and centre it over the mark on the paper. Now make a mark on the tissue paper at either end of the cardboard tube.

8. Measure 2in (5cm) away from either end of the cardboard tube and make more marks – the space between these marks represents the gap between the tubes where the cracker will be pinched in and tied.

9. Align the two smaller tubes against the last marks and make another mark at the end of each.

10. Keeping the tubes almost in position, run a little hot glue along the edge of the pink paper between the marks where the large centre tube will be. Roll the tube on to it and hold in place until it is stuck. Repeat the process for the two smaller tubes, remembering to leave the gaps.

11. Roll the cracker up firmly. Secure it with a line of hot glue along the cracker, ½in (1.5cm) inside the open scalloped edges of paper. Hold firmly in position until stuck.

12. Cut two lengths of narrow braid or ribbon. Tie one length around one end of the cracker in the gap between the lengths of tube. Pull tight, tie into a bow and trim the ends with scissors. Insert a small gift in the other end of the cracker, before tying the second length of braid or ribbon in a bow. If the tissue paper ends of the cracker look a little unbalanced, adjust them now by cutting.

13. Hot glue a dried rose into the centre of the bow at each end of the cracker. Finally, carefully attach a scattering of rose petals to the handmade paper with tiny blobs of glue.

Old-fashioned Christmas stockings

Any small pieces of fabric, together with odd buttons, tassels and remnants of braid, can be used to make these Christmas Eve stockings (see also page 49). If your piece of fabric is long enough, the boots can be made without a seam between shoe and leg.

You will need

Paper and pencil
Scissors
Long glass-headed pins
Suitable fabric
Sewing machine or needle and thread
Sari braid
Cotton wadding
Wooden spoon
Decorative tassels, braid or buttons
Cord or ribbon

1. Draw the required template(s) on paper. Draw a shoe shape, making it larger all round than the required finished size to allow for seams. Then draw the leg of the boot and cut out the two templates. (Make just one template if you have enough fabric to cut the whole stocking shape in a single piece.)

2. Fold your fabric in half, right sides together. Pin the patterns on the fabric and cut two shapes of each shoe and leg piece.

3. With the fabric right sides facing, pin together the two sides of the leg piece and pin all around the shoe piece, leaving the top of the shoe open. Machine or hand stitch the seams.

4. Turn both pieces the right side out. Cut a piece of sari braid to fit the opening at the top of the stocking. With right sides together, pin then stitch the braid to the top of the leg piece. Turn the braid in to conceal the raw edges at the top of the boot and catch it to the fabric with a few neat stitches. Turn the piece inside out once more, so that the wrong side of the fabric is facing outwards.

5. Slip the unbraided end of the leg shape over the shoe, so that the raw edges meet and the right sides of fabric are together. Pin then stitch the two pieces together. Turn the now complete stocking the right side out.

6. Stuff the foot of the stocking with the wadding, using the handle of a wooden spoon to fill the heel and toe. Mould into a realistic shape. Sew across the top of the shoe if you prefer to contain the wadding.

7. Decorate the stocking with any suitable tassels, braid and buttons. Use more braid to mask the seam where the shoe and leg pieces are joined, if you like. If the stocking is to be suspended from a hook, attach a loop of cord or ribbon to the top with a few stitches.

8. Fill the stocking with goodies and hang it up.

Fabulous packaging

Exquisitely wrapped gifts add a magical touch to Christmas. These shimmering silvery parcels are a pleasant change from the mundane shop-bought giftwrap. Similarly, why spend a fortune on buying Christmas giftbags when you can make your own? You can have such fun wrapping presents and the highlight will be the enjoyment of giving!

DECADENT PACKAGING

You will need

Sheets of frosted, opalescent and glittering tissue papers (see page 88)
Hot glue gun and glue stick or double-sided tape
Roll of clear cellophane
Silver-coloured wide wire-edged sheer or metallic ribbon
Decorations such as glass or plastic "crystals", beads or "jewels", silk cord tassels or a few pressed dried leaves, sprayed silver (see page 16)
Gift tags
Silver embroidery thread

If the gift to be wrapped is an odd shape, try to find a box in which it can fit snugly since it is easier to wrap regular shapes.

1. Wrap the present in your decorated tissue paper and secure the ends with a spot of hot glue or double-sided tape.

2. Overwrap the parcel with clear cellophane, again securing the ends with a little glue. Tie a generous length of ribbon around the parcel, in an extravagant bow.

3. Decorate with crystals, beads, tassels, or silver-sprayed leaves. Attach home-made gift tags with silver metallic embroidery thread to finish.

GIFT TAGS

Have a go at making your own gift tags. They can be single pieces of art paper – thick art paper or a lovely soft white art paper with a watermark look good, while ordinary thick cartridge paper is suitable for painting. If you prefer plain gift tags, overlay them with pieces of very textured see-through coloured paper, tissue paper, or even very fine fabric.

Use pinking shears or paper edge-cutters for attractive edges or tear the papers by carefully pulling the paper upwards against the edge of the ruler so that it tears in a neat line.

More ideas can be found on page 38 (Painted Cards in Purples & Pinks), which can easily be adapted to gift tags. Attaching one or two plastic "crystals" all adds to the shimmery appearance.

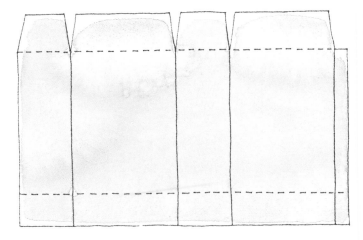

ALL BAGGED UP

You will need

1 sheet of thick coloured paper
Pencil
Ruler
Scissors
Craft knife
Double-sided tape, paper glue
*   or hot glue gun and*
*   glue stick*
Clothes peg
Jam jar with lid
Artist's concentrated liquid
*   colour in medium magenta*
*   and interference*
*   (opalescent) violet*
Nos. 5, 6 or 7 artist's
*   paintbrush*
Roll of clear cellophane
Narrow curling ribbon
Gift tags (see previous page)
Hole punch and silk cord or
*   rope for handles (optional)*
Plastic stars, "crystals" or
*   "jewels"*

The sizes of these bags are entirely up to you. Just follow the given pattern as a guide and adjust the measurements as required.

Cellophane works well for overwrapping, especially over the opalescent paint, as it shows the pearly finish to great advantage. It is also perfect for tying bows because it is soft to work with but crisp enough to hold its shape.

1. Spread out your sheet of paper on a flat work surface. Decide on the size – the height and width – required for your bag and draw the pattern accordingly, using a pencil and ruler.

2. Cut out your bag and score along the fold lines using a craft knife. Fold the paper inwards along the scored lines.

3. To make up the bag, use double-sided tape to stick the side tab to the side edge, or use glue and hold in place with a clothes peg until firmly stuck.

4. Fold in the base flaps and secure in the same way.

5. Fill the jam jar with water. Shake the containers of liquid paint and squeeze a little of each colour on to the jar lid to use it as a palette.

6. Dip your paintbrush in the water and use a minimal amount of water to thin the paint slightly and mix the two colours together. Paint a design of circles, squiggles or whatever else you like on the sides of the bag. Leave to dry thoroughly for about 1 hour.

7. Cut a long piece of cellophane to wrap around the bag. Tuck the top edge in over the top of the bag and secure with glue or tape. Cut long narrow strips of cellophane, bunch them together and tie or glue on to the bag for extra effect.

8. Tie narrow curling ribbon around the bag to close it, if liked, and attach a gift tag. Alternatively, you could punch holes near the top of the bag and thread silk cord or rope through the holes to make handles for the bag. Add plastic stars, "crystals" or "jewels" to decorate, pop your present inside and enjoy giving it to someone special.

PLEATED TISSUE PAPER PACKAGING

This eye-catching packaging is simple to make. Either wrap the gift in tissue paper first, or cover a box (lid and base separately) in slightly different colours of the same shade, then pleat another sheet of tissue paper to decorate the package.

Begin pleating from one corner of a sheet of tissue paper, making fairly narrow pleats. Work gradually, checking that you are still pleating in a straight line. Once you begin, you will see all sorts of possibilities, such as folding the pleated paper back on itself, or bending it around the corner of the present.

Stick it in place with paper glue or hot glue. Decorate the package further with a tissue paper flower (see page 117) or with silver- or gold-sprayed pressed dried autumn leaves (see page 16) or any other decorations that you like.

Decorations with a difference

Clementine "trees" set in bronzed urns make extremely stylish formal-looking decorations. The festive vibrant orange against the rich green of the foliage is both unusual and attractive. Similarly, a clever arrangement of gilded frames displaying pictures of angels makes a stunning seasonal statement.

CLEMENTINE "TREES"

You will need

2 concrete or plastic urns
Old spoon
Matt emulsion paint in black
    or dark grey, and brown
Plastic carton
Small bristle brush or fitch
1in (2.5cm) household
    paintbrush (optional)
Liberon gilt cream (Rambouillet)
Stones or sand (for plastic
    urns)
Hot glue gun and glue stick
2 dry oasis (dry florist's foam)
    cones at least as tall as
    the urns and of a diameter
    to just fit inside them, or
    chicken wire and large
    blocks of dry oasis to
    make your own cones
    (see below)
Sprigs of sweet bay, rosemary,
    pine, box or camellia
Secateurs
Lengths of thick florist's wire
    (1 stem for each fruit)
Approx. 40 clementines or
    satsumas per tree

These formal arrangements are ideal for display on a sideboard or a serving table. If you are making small trees in much smaller containers, cocktail sticks could be used instead of wire to fix the fruit to the dry oasis.

Dry oasis cones are available from large craft suppliers or florists. Alternatively, you could make a "cage" from chicken wire and shape it into a pointed cone to encase a large block of dry oasis. Make sure you cut a piece of dry oasis for the very top and pack the cage full.

1. First paint the urns. If concrete, spoon some of the black or dark grey emulsion paint into a plastic carton (if you dip the brush directly into the tin of paint you may leave behind loose gritty pieces from the concrete surface). Using a small bristle brush or fitch, stipple the paint into the rough surfaces of the concrete urns all over, inside and out.

2. Transfer a little of the brown paint to the carton. Then, without washing the paintbrush first, stipple the brown paint over the urns in patches, inside and out, until the concrete colour of the background has been completely covered. Repeat the process for a good dark depth of cover, deliberately making some patches darker than others. Leave to dry.

3. If your urns are plastic, take a household paintbrush and paint them all over, inside and out, with the black paint until the urns are totally covered. Leave to dry. Before applying a second coat of paint, turn the urns upside down and cover any

overlooked areas. Ensure the urns have a good dense covering of paint all over. Leave to dry.

4. Complete the plastic urns by stippling patches of colour over the base coat. Using the bristle brush, and with the brown and black tins of paint in front of you, stipple the colours in patches, switching from one to the other without cleaning the brush, until the surface takes on a more uneven appearance. Let the paint dry partially before stippling the whole surface again, this time being a little more generous with the black paint. Leave to dry.

5. Next, using the cleaned dry bristle brush, apply gilt cream to your plastic or concrete painted urns – as generously or sparsely as you wish. Leave to dry.

6. If using plastic urns, place stones or sand in the base to prevent them toppling over.

7. Apply plenty of hot glue inside the rim of each urn and sit the base of a dry oasis cone on it, pressing down firmly until stuck. If you are using a wire cage filled with oasis, crush and bend the wire to fit into, or slightly over, the rim of the urn. Hot glue the wire to the urn and hold in place until firmly stuck. Any protruding pieces of wire can be bent as far out of sight as possible; the rest will be masked by the greenery.

8. Start pushing the sprigs of greenery into the dry oasis to cover the cones – and any wire or glue that is showing – completely. Trim any stray bits of foliage with the secateurs as you work.

9. Pass a length of thick florist's wire through the bottom half of each clementine or satsuma, and twist the ends of wire together. Push the wires through the foliage into the dry oasis cones. Stand back for a last check that no wire or oasis is visible and that the fruit looks balanced. If not, move one or two until you are satisfied with the effect.

WALL OF ANGELS

This stunning arrangement of gilded frames displaying pictures of angels is a simple way to create the atmosphere of

Christmas and is a little more unusual than many festive decorations. It is particularly suited to a room lit only by candlelight, such as a hallway or dining room.

Save and collect any small picture frames, which can be transformed in minutes with a lick of paint, or a quick rub of gilt cream. Cut pictures of angels from last year's Christmas cards and pop them inside the frames.

Knock in a few small panel or picture pins and hang your pictures. Spray a metal sconce with gold paint, light the candles and there you have your wall display just for Christmas.

Morning makeovers

Try something new this Christmas, be it weaving an elegant garland or wreath of greenery or painting glass baubles to hang on the tree. Spray dried leaves with gold or silver to make stunning "trees", decorate baskets for special presents, or add a sealing wax stamp for the finishing touch to a personal gift. The main thing is to have fun and enjoy the projects.

Hand-painted glass baubles

Have a go at making your own unique Christmas tree decorations in the colours of your choice. You will need to seek out the clear glass baubles; the glass paints and relief outliner are readily available (see page 106).

PAINTED BAUBLES

You will need

Clear glass baubles
Fine artist's paintbrushes
Solvent-based glass paints (such as
   Vitrail) in lime green, carmine,
   violet and turquoise
Appropriate thinner or white spirit
Kitchen paper
Egg carton or small jam jars
Gold relief outliner (contour paste)
Pin
Cotton bud
Scissors
Thin cord or ribbon

Clear glass baubles are available from some of the bigger super-markets, large garden centres, good department stores and large craft suppliers.

The best way to hold a bauble for painting is with your middle finger at the top and your thumb at the bottom. If you prefer, stand the baubles in an egg carton or on top of a small jam jar.

Paint half the bauble and leave it to dry overnight; paint the other half the next day. Alternatively thread a length of string through the loop at the top of the bauble and hang it up. Hold it as described, and paint the whole of one side (top and bottom), leaving it to dry overnight before painting the rest.

1. Carefully wash the baubles to remove any greasy fingermarks and dust and leave to dry.

2. Using a fine paintbrush and starting with the lime green glass paint, paint small diamond shapes on the baubles. Rinse the brush in the appropriate thinner or white spirit and dry it on kitchen paper in between colours. The paint is touch dry after about 1 hour.

3. Repeat the process with the carmine paint, then the violet and lastly the turquoise paint. Leave overnight to dry completely.

4. Unscrew the cap from the tube of gold relief outliner and pierce the nozzle with a pin to ensure a fine line of paste will be released. Carefully outline each painted diamond shape with the outliner by placing the tip lightly on the surface of the bauble and squeezing gently and evenly while pulling the tube along the surface. Wipe away any mistakes immediately with a cotton bud. Leave the baubles for at least 1 hour to allow the relief outliner to dry.

5. To finish the baubles, cut lengths of pretty thin cord or ribbon and thread them through each bauble eyelet so that they can be hung up.

STONE-EMBELLISHED BAUBLES

In addition to the previous materials you will need yellow glass paint, ten $^3/_{10}$in (7.5mm) tiny topaz-coloured circular flat-backed acrylic jewels per bauble and two-part epoxy glue.

1. Prepare the baubles as before, ensuring the glass is clean.

2. To paint the top and bottom of the baubles, stand each one on top of a small jam jar. With its base uppermost, paint a large yellow star shape over the base.

Continue the design beyond the star, working down the bauble and using turquoise, green and violet paints in bands of colour. When the bauble is half finished and you have painted as far as you can reach, leave overnight to dry completely before turning it the right way up on the jam jar.

3. Repeat your design, again working down the bauble until the two halves of painted colour meet in the middle. Leave to dry for 1 hour.

4. Outline the star shapes at each end of each bauble using gold relief outliner. Leave to dry for at least 1 hour.

5. Prepare the epoxy glue according to the manufacturer's instructions and dab a little glue on to the back of each topaz-coloured stone. Press it lightly on to the glass surface at equal intervals around the middle of the bauble. The glue will dry clear.

6. Leave the baubles overnight to dry thoroughly, hanging them by cord or ribbon from a coat hanger in a place where the air can circulate around them.

PAINTED CHANDELIER PRISMS

You will need

Glass chandelier prisms
Solvent-based glass paints (such as Vitrail) in turquoise, violet, carmine, warm green and reseda
Appropriate thinner or white spirit
Fine artist's paintbrush
Kitchen paper
Scissors
Thin cord or ribbon

1. For a multi-coloured prism, begin by painting it with the turquoise glass paint, picking out some of the geometric facets with the colour. As always, rinse the brush in the appropriate thinner or white spirit and dry it on kitchen paper before moving on to the next colour.

2. Proceed in the same way, working with violet paint on some of the remaining facets. Pick out the final facets with carmine and hang the prism to dry overnight.

3. Take another prism and paint it with two shades of green, leaving some clear areas of glass. Paint two opposing sides of a four-faceted prism with reseda and the remaining two sides with warm green. Leave to dry.

4. The following day, repeat the whole process, applying a second coat of paint to each painted facet to give the prisms a much more intense and rich colour.

5. Leave to dry overnight, then thread with thin cord or ribbon.

Mantel garland

Adorn your fireplace with a garland using lots of fresh foliage, combined with silk flowers and silver-sprayed leaves and cones, dressed with elegant white ribbons. Used thoughtfully, a combination of silk flowers and rich green foliage can look sophisticated and lovely, giving your home a truly festive look.

You will need

Sheets of newspaper
Can of florist's silver metallic
    spray paint
Pair of lightweight disposable gloves
Larch cones on their stems
Lengths of ivy
Good selection of greenery, such
    as holly, ivy, leylandii, cherry
    laurel, eucalyptus
Secateurs
Spool of florist's thin wrapping wire
White silk roses
Hot glue gun and glue stick
Approx. 2¼ yd (2m) length of wide,
    wire-edged white silk ribbon
Reusable adhesive or masking tape

1. Spread out sheets of newspaper in a well-ventilated space suitable for spraying. Take the can of spray paint and shake it well for a couple of minutes before beginning, and remember to keep shaking it in between spraying.

2. Wearing the disposable gloves, so that you can hold the tips of the items while they are being sprayed, spray the larch cones and some lengths of ivy with the silver paint and set aside to dry.

3. Prepare the other greenery by cutting it into lengths of about 8in (20cm), using secateurs. Strip away the leaves from the base of each stem.

4. Take three lengths of assorted greenery and overlap the stems slightly. Wrap the spool of thin wire around and around the greenery, passing it carefully through the leaves, to hold the stems together. Extend the length of the garland by continually adding more greenery, wrapping steadily until the stems hold firmly together.

5. Use the wire to fix white silk roses to the length of greenery at intervals of about 12in (30cm). Attach silver-sprayed larch cones on their stems at intervals in the same way. Continue until the garland is of a length to match approximately half the width of your mantel, shelf or beam above the fireplace. Finish by wrapping the wire round and round the stems and passing it through to the back of the garland.

6. Repeat this process to make an identical length of wired greenery, adorned with silk roses and silver larch cones. When the second length is complete, wire the two together firmly to make one long garland.

7. Hot glue more silk roses in the centre of the garland, with extra green and silver-sprayed ivy. Try the garland on the mantel to check it looks fairly symmetrical. Remove it from the mantel and add long trailing lengths of ivy to the ends, securing them with wire and/or hot glue.

8. Finish by tying large voluptuous bows of white, wide wire-edged silk ribbon on the garland, teasing the long ribbon tails into attractive shapes and trimming them into inverted "V" shapes. Take great care to ensure that the garland is safely secured in place on the mantel – reusable adhesive or masking tape can be used and easily concealed beneath the garland.

Christmas wreaths

The delicate grey-green of eucalyptus provides a perfect background for silver-sprayed cape gooseberry pods, silver oak leaves, colourful frosted glass baubles and frothy ribbon. For a simpler effect, team holly, ivy, laurel or other evergreen foliage with simple gingham ribbon and natural products such as berries or apples.

EUCALYPTUS WREATH

You will need

Sheets of newspaper
Can of florist's silver metallic spray paint
Pair of lightweight disposable gloves
Cape gooseberry (physalis) pods
Pressed dried oak leaves
Secateurs
Eucalyptus foliage
Spool of florist's thin wrapping wire
Wire ring base
Pliers
Small white silk flowers on wire stems
Hot glue gun and glue stick
Frosted glass baubles
Florist's wire
Wide, wire-edged silver ribbon, plus extra ribbon for hanging the wreath
Scissors

1. Spread out sheets of newspaper in a well-ventilated space suitable for spraying. Take the can of spray paint and shake it well for a couple of minutes before beginning, and remember to keep shaking it in between spraying.

2. Wearing the disposable gloves, so that you can hold the tips of the items while they are being sprayed, spray the Cape gooseberry pods and dried oak leaves with the silver paint and leave to dry.

3. Using secateurs, cut the eucalyptus foliage into lengths of about 8in (20cm). Strip away the leaves from the base of each length to leave a stripped stem of about 2in (5cm) long.

4. Place the pieces of foliage one on top of the other, overlapping the stems slightly. Wire the cut pieces of eucalyptus together and wrap them around the wire ring by passing the spool of wire carefully between the leaves. If you have any variegated foliage, weave it in at intervals of 8in (20cm) or so. Continue until the wire ring base is completely covered with foliage.

5. Using secateurs or pliers, cut the stems of the individual white silk flowers into lengths of 6in (15cm) and 8in (20cm). Positioning the silk flowers at regular intervals around the ring, hot glue their stems and push them firmly into the foliage.

6. Wire the baubles carefully by cutting the florist's wire into 4in (10cm) lengths and threading a length through the loop on the top of each bauble. Bend the wire in half before twisting the ends together to secure. Place hot glue on the ends of the wire then push into the foliage stems to secure, positioning the baubles evenly around the ring.

7. Use hot glue to stick the silver-sprayed Cape gooseberry pods and oak leaves at intervals around the ring.

8. To complete the wreath, tie a generous length of wire-edged silver ribbon in a decorative bow. To attach the bow to the wreath, thread a length of florist's wire through the back loop of the bow knot, bend it in half and twist to secure before attaching it to the wreath. Trim the ends of the ribbon and shape the tails into inverted "V"s for extra effect.

9. Hang the wreath with another length of ribbon. To keep the wreath's greenery looking fresh for as long as possible, spray it occasionally with water using a fine plant spray.

TRADITIONAL FRONT DOOR WREATH

You will need

Wet oasis (wet florist's foam) ring, approx. 15–16in (38–40cm) diameter
Florist's or garden wire
Secateurs
Good selection of greenery, such as ivy, variegated ivy, holly, Portuguese or cherry laurel, bay, hebe or any other variegated leaves available
White plastic hellebore flowers
Bright red real or plastic berries or apples
Scissors
2yd (2m) length of wire-edged red/white checked ribbon

Although the wet oasis ring is backed with plastic, once you have soaked it in water it needs to be kept on a polythene sheet while you are working on it. Cut a good selection of greenery – you will need more than you imagine! Plastic flowers are available from florists, craft suppliers, large garden centres, some department stores and cut-price shops.

1. Start by soaking the wet oasis ring in lukewarm water for about 5 minutes. Remove from the water and place on your work surface.

2. Cut a length of florist's or garden wire and pass it around the wet oasis. Twist the ends together to make a loop by which to hang the wreath.

3. Using secateurs, cut the greenery into lengths of about 4–6in (10–15cm). Strip the stems slightly and push all the greenery into the wet oasis, using enough greenery so as to create a really full look.

4. Push the white flowers into the wet oasis, interspersed with the red berries or apples.

5. Cut the ribbon into two lengths and tie each into a bow, leaving the tails long. Thread a piece of wire through the back of the bow knot, twisting the ends together and cutting the wire to leave enough to push into the wet oasis at the top and bottom of the wreath. Bend the bow into a pleasing shape and trim the tail ends.

6. Watch for the water which will stream out when you lift the wreath to hang it on your door!

The feminine touch

Pretty, feminine presents are always a delight to make. This mirror, painted silver and decorated with dried rosebuds, is great fun and probably something you will either love or loathe! Glass painting is another popular option (see pages 102–7), while the frosted glassware overleaf is lovely and very simple to achieve with a can of spray.

ROSEBUD SILVER MIRROR

You will need

Small inexpensive softwood "tip" mirror
Scissors
Scrap paper
Low-contact masking tape
Can of florist's silver metallic spray paint, or silver gilt cream plus small paintbrush, white spirit and soft cloth
Silver relief outliner (contour paste)

1–2 packets of dried rosebuds
Hot glue gun and glue stick
2 pressed dried leaves, sprayed silver (see page 16)
Pearl beads and other suitable decorations
Glass-beaded and/or cotton key tassels
Silk ribbon rose (see page 14)

I had such fun with this piece. It is very different, very feminine, a little crazy and eccentric (like me)

but fun to make and use. If it collects dust after constant use you can always aim a cool hairdryer at it, and if it finally becomes too shabby, it can be undone, and you will have the mirror to begin again with another theme. (See page 32 for another feminine present idea that uses dried rosebuds.)

1. Carefully clean the mirror well to remove greasy fingermarks and dust and leave to dry.

2. Cut a piece of scrap paper slightly smaller than the mirror glass. Using low-contact masking tape stick the paper carefully inside the mirror frame to protect the glass while you paint the frame silver.

3. Take the can of spray paint, if using, and shake it well for a couple of minutes before spraying the whole of the mirror frame and stand silver. Alternatively, apply silver gilt cream using a small paintbrush and thinning the cream a little with white spirit so that it is easier to apply. Leave to dry thoroughly. If using gilt cream, buff with a soft cloth when dry for a shiny finish.

4. Remove the paper and masking tape from the glass. Using the edge of the frame as a guide, draw another "frame" inside it on the glass with the silver relief outliner. Fill this border with decorative silver squiggles, scrolls and circles. Leave for at least 1 hour to dry.

5. Open the packet of dried rosebuds and sort them by size. Hot glue a few rosebuds on to the silver frame at each corner of the mirror. Build up an attractive shape as you work by using larger rosebuds in the middle and tiny ones on the end (see main picture).

6. Tuck silver-sprayed leaves behind the rosebuds and glue the ends of their stems to the mirror

frame. Hot glue the pearl beads and any other suitable decorations to the glass, taking care not to burn your fingers.

7. Finish by gluing tassels either side of the mirror and a silk ribbon rose on one side.

FROSTED GLASS

You will need

Assorted glassware, such as
*   bowls, tall bottles, votive*
*   candle holders, ordinary*
*   tumblers or wine glasses*
Low-contact masking tape
Can of etched glass/frosting
*   spray paint*
Silver relief outliner
*   (contour paste)*

The glass items used here came from a charity shop and a jumble sale. The can of spray for frosted and etched glass worked very well for me. The spray is easy to use and produces a lovely effect.

Do make sure you read the manufacturer's instructions first for the best results.

1. Carefully wash the glass items well to remove any greasy fingermarks and dust, then leave to dry before proceeding.

2. To create your design, apply strips of low-contact masking tape to the areas of the glass that you want left clear.

3. Take the can of spray paint and read the instructions. Shake it well for a couple of minutes before beginning. Working in a well-ventilated space, spray the glass well then leave to dry. For a denser frosted effect, apply a second coat once the first coat is dry. Leave to dry.

4. Remove the masking tape. Outline the design using a fine silver relief outliner, or draw a design of flowers on the frosted glass, as you prefer. Leave to dry.

Gilded leaf trees

These stunning gilded leaf trees make good use of fallen leaves gathered during the autumn when dry and then pressed between the pages of a substantial book for a few weeks to flatten them. Try to find lots of leaves of the same species to make large projects in a uniform shape.

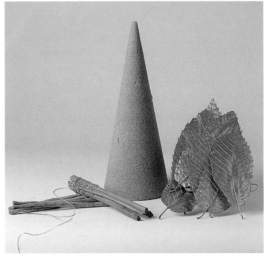

GOLDEN HAZEL LEAF TREE

You will need

Small straight-sided terracotta
*   flowerpot*
White spirit
Jam jar
Small paintbrush
Kitchen paper or a rag
Liberon gilt cream (Versailles)
Acrylic gold size
Scissors
2–3 sheets of Dutch metal
*   transfer leaf*
Soft brush
Craft knife

Small block of dry oasis
*   (dry florist's foam), plus a*
*   9in (23cm) tall dry oasis*
*   (dry florist's foam) cone*
3–4 sturdy, straight
*   cinnamon sticks*
Gold metallic thread or fine wire
Pressed dried leaves, sprayed
*   gold (see page 16)*
Hot glue gun and glue stick
Dried lichen or tiny larch cones
Gold-coloured wire-edged
*   ribbon*

1. If the flowerpot is old, scrub it clean and leave to dry out well, remembering that terracotta is porous.

2. Pour a small quantity of white spirit into a jam jar. Dip a small paintbrush into the white spirit then wipe most of it off on kitchen paper or a rag and use the brush to apply the gilt cream to the terracotta pot – the white spirit will thin the gilt cream to give it a consistency more like paint, which can then be spread evenly. Brush it inside the pot at the top as well. Leave for about 1 hour to dry.

3. Using the same paintbrush, now cleaned, brush the gold size on to the pot in vertical stripes. Leave for at least 15 minutes until the gold size is tacky.

4. Cut the transfer leaf into strips to apply to the gold-sized areas. Gently press each strip on to the gold size, smoothing your fingers over the sheet until all of the leaf has transferred to the surface of the pot. Remove the backing tissue. Continue until all the stripes are done. Use a soft brush gently over the pot to remove any excess metal leaf.

SILVER OAK LEAF TREE

Create a similar tree in silver, this time using oak leaves. Take a can of florist's silver metallic spray paint and shake it well for a couple of minutes before use – remember to keep shaking it in between spraying. Working in a well-ventilated space, spray your scrubbed terracotta pot and oak leaves with the paint and leave them to dry, before making the "tree" as before.

Hot glue a few decorations to the silver pot, for example glass nuggets, flat-backed acrylic jewels, round and heart-shaped silver sequins.

5. Cut the block of dry oasis into a piece to fit snugly into the pot and press into place. Tie the cinnamon sticks firmly together with gold metallic thread or fine wire, then push them down into the centre of the pot.

6. Push the dry oasis cone on to the cinnamon sticks, making sure the cone is central and level.

7. Beginning at the base of the cone and progressing around it, hot glue the top half of each leaf to the cone, applying the glue generously until the first, bottom layer is complete. Continue working up the cone, gluing leaves in layers until it is completely covered, saving three or four small beautifully shaped leaves for the top.

8. Sprinkle lichen or tiny larch cones loosely around the base of the cinnamon sticks to cover the top of the dry oasis. To complete the tree tie a length of ribbon in a bow around the cinnamon sticks below the cone and trim the ends of the ribbon into inverted "V" shapes.

Stylish stamped stationery

This is a fun project for the whole family! Cut potatoes into shapes to stamp writing paper, cards, gift tags, invitations and giftwrap for a stunning hand-printed look. Simple mosaic-style shapes like squares, triangles, diamonds and circles work best.

You will need

Ruler and pencil

Long-bladed scissors and small sharp scissors

Sheets of assorted paper and/or card in various types, weights, textures and colours

Sharp vegetable knife

Large baking potatoes

Black felt-tip pen

Kitchen paper

Artist's acrylic tube paints (or matt emulsion paint) in Indo orange red, cadmium red light and medium, Venetian red, raw sienna, burnt sienna, raw umber, yellow ochre, crimson and rich gold

Jam jar lid

Small paintbrush or flat fitch

No. 4 artist's paintbrush

Hole punch

String or ribbon

Brown card labels for gift tags (optional)

Bulldog clips or strong clothes pegs

It is a good idea to practise cutting the potatoes and experiment with different shapes of stamp on scrap paper before starting the real thing.

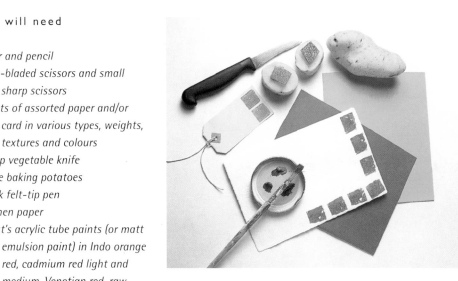

1. Cut your paper or card and fold to make the size of greeting cards and gift tags required.

2. Halve a potato using a sharp knife and cut a slice off the base so that it will stand level. Using a black felt-tip pen, draw your chosen shape on the cut potato, which will be wet. Some shapes work better than others and it is best to start with simple ones first, such as triangles, simple squares, diamonds and octagons. You can experiment later with simple leaf and berry shapes, stars or flowers.

3. Using the sharp knife, cut downwards around the shape following the felt-tip outline. Then slice into the side of the potato carefully to meet the vertical cuts; remove the excess potato around the "stamp" you have created. Pat the cut surfaces of potato dry with kitchen paper.

4. Squeeze a little of your chosen paints on to a jar lid "palette". Load the potato stamp evenly with paint, using a small paintbrush or flat fitch, then press it on your chosen surface to produce a sharply defined image.

5. To vary your designs you could paint a border around some cards using a small artist's paintbrush. Allow to dry before stamping a design on top. Another option is to pick out the edges of cards in rich gold paint. For some designs, for example borders, it is easier to first draw fine straight pencil lines as a guide to keep within.

8. Leave the stamped stationery to dry on a flat surface or make string "clothes lines" and attach the stationery to the string with bulldog clips or clothes pegs.

9. Punch holes in your gift tags and thread with string or ribbon. (Alternatively, use ready-made plain brown parcel labels as tags.)

10. If you like, cut leaves, bows or other shapes out of thick coloured art paper and stick on the stationery as extra decoration. Once you are inspired, you could use potato stamps to cover an album, make a cookery book cover, or cover a journal or address book, all of which would make acceptable and unusual Christmas presents.

Decorated baskets

With the advent of plastic bags came the demise of basket weaving, and lovely old baskets have been hard to find. However, this ancient craft is now enjoying a great revival and the market is flooded with cheap imports, many of which are exceptionally attractive and widely available. They make ideal gifts filled with flowers or house plants, candles, soaps and home-made preserves.

HESSIAN-LINED BASKET

You will need

Small tall-handled basket
Tape measure
Scissors
Jute hessian, plus extra loose hessian to pack between gifts
Large-eyed, blunt-ended needle, such as a tapestry needle
Jute string

Jute hessian and jute string are both available from good garden centres. If the basket is to be used for plants or a flower arrangement it is best to line it with a piece of thick polythene or oilcloth to stop any water seeping out. If this is the case, you need only decorate the rim of the basket with hessian.

1. To cover the basket rim only with hessian, measure the circumference of your basket and cut a long strip of hessian to length, plus a little extra for overlapping. The strip should be double, or even treble, thickness, so that it can be folded edges to the middle, or rolled over two or three times, to provide a substantial thickness. It should overlap the edge of the rim of the basket by about 1in (2.5cm) both inside and out.

2. Thread the needle with jute string and tie a knot in the end – this can be hidden underneath the hessian to begin. Stitch the hessian over the basket rim, working in an over-and-over cross-stitch, passing the needle through the basket to the front, over the top and through the basket again to the front. When you have worked your way around the rim, secure the string with a few stitches on the inside of the basket and cut.

3. To line the whole basket, lay the piece of hessian inside the basket. Push it down into the bottom and allow it to drape over the outside of the basket on to the work surface. Trim the hessian all the way round, until it hangs about 1in (2.5cm) above the work surface.

4. Anchor the hessian with a few stitches around the inside of the base of the basket. Fold, or loosely roll the hessian from the raw cut edge inwards and upwards until the band of excess hessian is about 2–3in (5–7.5cm) wide and can overlap the edge of the rim of the basket by about 1in (2.5cm) both inside and out. Secure by overstitching around the rim of the basket as before. Use any remnants of hessian to pack between gifts in the basket.

LARCH CONE DECORATED BASKET

You will need

Small old willow basket
Long length of tartan or other festive ribbon
Hot glue gun and glue stick
Tiny larch cones
Vibrant coloured or crisp acid-free white tissue paper

1. Beginning at the bottom of one side of the handle, hot glue one end of a long length of ribbon to the handle. Bind the ribbon around the handle, working upwards and over the handle, wrapping it round and round neatly and firmly to cover the handle completely. When you reach the bottom of the other side of the handle, trim the ribbon and secure with glue as before. Tie more lengths of the same ribbon into two bows and stick each one on the outside of the basket at the base of the handle.

2. Hot glue the larch cones in two tightly packed rows around the top edge of the basket, filling in where necessary to improve the general appearance, or to hide blobs of glue.

3. Use small pieces of scrunched up tissue paper to pack between gifts placed in the basket.

CINNAMON "BASKET"

You will need

Sharp craft knife
Plastic plant pot
Packet of sturdy cinnamon sticks
Hot glue gun and glue stick
Scissors
Ribbon, rope or braid
Home-made or shop-bought seasonal pot-pourri

1. Using a sharp craft knife, cut down the plastic pot to measure a little less than the height of the cinnamon sticks when stood upright.

2. Trim the cinnamon sticks to one length. Using the cinnamon sticks vertically, hot glue them neatly around the side of the plant pot, filling any gaps with thin sticks, until the plastic is no longer visible.

3. Cut decorative ribbon, rope or braid to length and tie it around the cinnamon sticks, securing with glue if necessary. Fill the pot with seasonal pot-pourri.

GIFT FOR A GARDENER

For the basket of gardening goodies pictured above, select a fairly roomy "wild", rustic-looking basket from the baskets galore available in every garden centre, florist's and craft supplier and in many high-street stores.

If the present is for someone close to you, you will already know the items they particularly want; otherwise, long-lasting plant and seed labels, organic seeds, natural raffia, inexpensive secateurs, gardening gloves and lovely old terracotta pots will make a delightful gift for any keen gardener.

Floral giftwrapped soaps

Christmas wouldn't be Christmas without receiving something extravagant and delicious to use in the bath! Buy some beautiful handmade soaps and wrap them in your own stunning paper. If you prefer the packaging to look Christmassy, look for papers with Victorian-style festive images instead of the lovely floral patterns used here.

You will need

Cold tea and small paintbrush (optional)
2 sheets of different good-quality giftwrap, one with a small old-fashioned floral design, the other with subjects from nature (such as feathers, birds' eggs, shells, insects) or old script
Sheets of brown manila paper
Sheets of textured handmade paper
Iron (optional)
Small sharp scissors
Handmade soaps, such as violet, oatmeal, jojoba, eucalyptus, rose, evening primrose, and lavender
Narrow clear adhesive tape, or hot glue gun and glue stick
Paper edge-cutters (optional)
Remnants of filigree, metallic or sheer fabric, ribbon, cotton ricrac or lace, or lengths of jute string or natural raffia
Matches
Red or gold sealing wax and small sealing stamp

The desired effect here is a layered look. The soaps are wrapped in manila or textured handmade paper and then over-wrapped with a band of the more decorative paper. A remnant of fabric or ribbon and a little sealing wax completes the idea. Sealing wax and small sealing stamps are available from good stationers and some gift shops.

1. For an antique effect, brush cold tea over your chosen paper. Allow the paper to dry thoroughly. Good-quality paper should not be affected by the tea painting, but thinner paper may become uneven or slightly wrinkled, in which case iron it on the plain side when dry.

2. For smaller tablets of soap cut the handmade paper into pieces of a size to neatly package each bar. Wrap the lengths of paper around the tablets of soap simply as a wide band, leaving the ends of the soap exposed, or enclose them completely in the paper as you would wrap a parcel. Secure the paper with a tiny piece of clear adhesive tape or a small blob of hot glue.

3. Cut the same number of narrow bands from the floral wrapping paper, shaping the long edges of each strip of paper decoratively with scissors or paper edge-cutters. Wrap the bands of floral paper around the middle of the little packages of soap, over the handmade paper. Secure with adhesive tape or glue as before, at the back or underneath the soap.

4. Wrap the larger bath soaps in the manila paper first, enclosing them totally in the paper. Cut

the other sheet of giftwrap
into rectangles to overwrap the
manila, covering the full width
or length of the bars of soap and
overlapping underneath by about
1in (2.5cm). Secure as before.

5. Overwrap all the soaps with
short lengths of fabric or ribbon,

securing each with a knot. If
the soap is a gift for a man,
you may prefer to use a dark
metallic fabric or jute string
or natural raffia to tie up the
package. In contrast, decorate
the small tablets of soap more
delicately, using old lace or
sheer fabric.

6. Light the sealing wax
stick and allow it to drip into a
large blob on top of the knotted
fabric, ribbon or string before
pressing the stamp down for a
few seconds to make the seal.
Take care that the sealing wax
does not drip where it is not
wanted, and that it does not

smoke and make a horrid black
mess. This is usually caused by
holding the wax stick at an
angle, rather than upside down,
so that the flame burns the
wax away too quickly and the
wick begins to smoke. (Do keep
matches out of reach of
children.)

Evening escapades

With a spare evening in hand you might like to switch off from the day with one of these projects. Have a go at painting, sewing or gluing. Experiment with opalescent paints on tissue paper and create wonderful unique giftwrap. The painted glass projects are great fun to do and you'll find yourself running out of glass to paint! Sew silk velvet purses or little lavender bags, or make a "tree" of larch cones or fragrant dried rosebuds.

Frosted, opalescent & glittering tissue papers

Experiment with your own ideas, patterns and colours for these fabulous, highly unique tissue wrapping papers. Create cool, frosted and pearly finishes using opalescent liquid paints; abstract or geometric images or a design of icicles in shimmering silvery glitter. Finish them with sequins, pearls and sheesha glass.

STARS ON BLUE PEARLY TISSUE

You will need

1 sheet of pearly/metallic blue tissue paper
Artist's acrylic tube paint in magenta and light green
Plastic carton lid
Small artist's paintbrush
Star stamps in two different designs
Gold relief outliner (contour paste)

1. Spread out a sheet of pearly/metallic blue tissue paper on a flat work surface. Squeeze a little of each artist's acrylic tube paint on to the plastic carton lid, using it as a palette. Using a small artist's paintbrush, apply the magenta tube paint evenly to one of the star stamps.

2. Stamp a line of pink stars, about 6in (15cm) apart, all across the sheet of tissue paper, remembering to replenish the paint between each stamping.

3. Wash the paintbrush before applying light green paint to the other star stamp. Stamp green stars in the spaces between the pink ones, taking care not to smudge the pink stars. Leave to dry for 30 minutes.

4. To finish the paper, draw a spiral of gold in the centres of all the green stars using the gold relief outliner. (If you have to break the seal of the relief outliner yourself, make sure you do so with a pin to ensure that you have a fine nozzle to work with.) Leave the paper to dry overnight in a warm environment.

MAGENTA & BLUE STARS

A variation on this design is to use metallic blue tube paint instead of light green and to use silver relief outliner instead of gold for the centre of the stars. Leave to dry overnight.

1. Using only one of the star stamps, cover the pearly blue tissue paper with light green stars and leave to dry.

2. Prepare the epoxy glue according to the manufacturer's instructions. Apply glue to the back of each piece of mirror glass and press one firmly in the centre of each green star.

3. Outline each green star with silver relief outliner and leave to dry overnight.

GOLD STARS ON BLACK

You will need

1 sheet of black tissue paper
Artist's acrylic tube paint
*   in gold*
Jam jar lid
Small artist's paintbrush
Star stamp
Gold relief outliner
*   (contour paste)*

1. Spread out a sheet of black tissue paper on a flat work surface. Squeeze a little gold acrylic tube paint on to the jar lid palette. Using a small paintbrush, apply the paint evenly to the star stamp.

2. Stamp gold stars at random all over the sheet of tissue paper, replenishing the paint between each stamping. Leave to dry for 30 minutes.

3. Finish by using the gold relief outliner around each star and drawing a spiral of gold in the centre of each one. Leave the paper to dry overnight as before.

BLUE, MAGENTA & GREEN STARS

Another option is to vary the main design by introducing a third colour.

Having stamped the paper with stars in magenta and green paint, use metallic blue tube paint to stamp some more stars. Once the paint is completely dry, use silver glitter glue to partially outline the blue stars, occasionally accentuating the centre of a pink or green star. Leave the paper to dry overnight.

MIRRORED STARS

In addition to the previous materials used, this simple yet stunning design requires small round pieces of sheesha mirror glass (see page 110) and two-part epoxy glue.

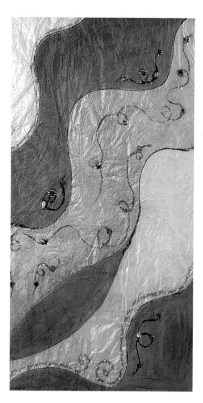

IRIDESCENT & PEARLY COLOURS ON WHITE TISSUE

You will need

2 sheets of crisp acid-free
    white tissue paper
Dark blue and dark green glitter
    glue (pen or applicator)
Jam jar with lid
Artist's concentrated liquid
    colour in green and
    interference (opalescent)
    green, brilliant purple and
    interference (opalescent)
    violet
½in (1.5cm) household
    paintbrush
Green sequins

You could use this first design as
an exercise to get your hand and
eye in, and to have fun

experimenting, before getting
down to the real thing. All of
the following painted tissue
projects require two sheets
(double thickness) of tissue paper
to achieve the effect. Also, since
the paint is used with water all
across the sheet, it tends to
stick the sheets together so is
necessary from a practical point
of view as well.

The artist's concentrated
liquid colours in the
"interference" range are usually
labelled "opalescent" or "opal"
as well, although the white is
labelled "iridescent/metallic/
pearlescent white" – just to be
confusing! All of these colours
can be mixed with artist's
acrylic tube paints, or painted
over them while they are still
wet. Use the relevant opalescent
colour with a solid colour – for
example interference

(opalescent) green with or
over any green tube paint. The
iridescent white, however, can
be added to – or painted over –
any colour.

1. Spread out the double
thickness of white tissue paper
on a flat work surface.

2. Shake the glitter glue
containers. If you have to break
the seal yourself, try not to
make the hole too large – just
large enough to allow the
particles of glitter to flow
through. Roughly draw the
outline and design pictured
(above left), using the dark blue
glitter glue pen. The glitter glue
will take at least 1 hour to dry
in a warm environment, but you
can still fill in the design with the
paint, as long as you stay within
the blue lines.

3. Fill the jam jar with water.
Shake the containers of liquid
paint and squeeze a little of each
of the two green colours on to
the jar lid to use it as a palette.

4. Moisten your paintbrush in
the water and mix the green
paint with a little of the
opalescent green. Paint the green
semi-circles at the ends of the
design. Add more opalescent
green to the paint and paint the
central circles, which are paler in
colour and more pearlescent.

5. Clean the brush and add
the remaining paints to the
palette. Mix only a tiny amount
of opalescent violet with the
brilliant purple. Paint the purple
areas of the design.

6. Finally, draw a few leaves
using the dark green glitter glue.

Lay a few deep green sequins on top for added sparkle. Leave to dry for 2–3 hours.

FROSTED ICICLES ON PINK

You will need

2 sheets of crisp acid-free white tissue paper
Silver glitter glue (pen or applicator)
Jam jar with lid
Artist's concentrated liquid colour in medium magenta, interference (opalescent) violet and iridescent white
½in (1.5cm) household paintbrush
½yd (0.5m) band of clear sequins
Pink, diamond-shaped self-adhesive stickers

This striking design of jagged icicles on a deep pink background is accentuated by the silvery frost effect outline and crystalline sequins. It makes a seasonally attractive, wintry looking paper, which shimmers magically when overwrapped with clear cellophane to reflect the light and the colours beneath.

1. Spread out the double thickness of white tissue paper on a flat work surface. Draw the outline of the frame and the icicles on the paper using the silver glitter glue. This will take at least 1 hour to dry but you can still fill in the design with the paint, as long as you stay within the glitter glue lines.

2. Fill the jam jar with water. Shake the containers of liquid paint and squeeze a little of each colour on to the jar lid to use it as a palette.

3. Moisten your small household paintbrush in the water and mix the magenta with a little of the opalescent violet paint. Use it to fill in the border around the design and some of the background between the icicles. Vary the shade of pink for the remainder of the background by adjusting the ratio of the magenta, water and opalescent violet. For the paler areas, use only opalescent violet with a little water; paint some of the icicles white, using the iridescent white liquid paint.

4. Remove the clear sequins from their thread and place them very carefully along the lines of glitter glue while still wet. Leave to dry overnight or for at least 2 hours in a warm place. Do check that the glue is dry, since glitter glues vary in their drying times and smudge easily.

5. Once the paper is completely dry, attach a few of the pink self-adhesive stickers to the triangle points to complete the design.

PURPLE & GOLD WITH PEARLS & SEQUINS

You will need

2 sheets of crisp acid-free white tissue paper
Dark blue, silver and gold glitter glue pens
Jam jar with lid
Artist's concentrated liquid colours in brilliant purple, interference (opalescent) violet, opalescent gold and iridescent white
Artist's acrylic tube paint in ultramarine blue and yellow ochre or raw sienna (optional)
½in (1.5cm) household paintbrush
String of plastic "pearls"
Gold and silver Indian sequin beads

The addition of sequins and pearls to this flowing and curvaceous design makes for a most sumptuous, expensive – and different – looking giftwrap.

1. Spread out the double thickness of white tissue paper on a flat work surface. Draw a design of simple wavy lines across the paper, within a frame, using the dark blue glitter glue pen, taking care not to smudge it as you work. As before, you can proceed with filling in the design with paint, as long as you stay within the glitter glue lines.

2. Fill the jam jar with water. Shake the containers of liquid paint and squeeze a little of each colour on to the jar lid palette.

3. Moisten your paintbrush in the water and mix the brilliant purple with a little of the ultramarine blue tube paint. Use it to paint the frame of the design, roughly blending the colours with bold brushstrokes. Add a little opalescent violet to the paint and use it to paint some of the purple-coloured sections within the frame.

4. Paint another section with opalescent violet mixed with a little water only, and two other sections in iridescent white only.

5. Paint the central section with a mixture of yellow ochre tube paint and opalescent gold.

6. Draw curling silver lines on the two iridescent white painted sections with the silver glitter glue. Cut up the pearls and place them on the lines of glue.

7. Draw a few squiggly lines on the central gold-painted section with the gold glitter glue pen, and one or two lines of dark blue glitter glue on the purple-painted sections.

8. Place the relevant-coloured sequin beads on these glue lines. Leave the paper to dry overnight.

TURQUOISE BLUE & WHITE GEOMETRIC

This is another simple yet effective pattern, drawn freehand with a silver glitter glue applicator. Use artist's concentrated liquid colours in permanent light blue and iridescent white, using them together and separately for interest and variation. A scattering of clear sequins along the glue lines helps further reflect the light.

To see the effect when overwrapped with clear cellophane, turn to Fabulous Packaging (see page 60).

Silk velvet purses

The wintry white light reflects upon these sumptuously soft silk velvet purses, the subtly muted rich colours of which are enhanced by the unusual decorations, making them luxuriously desirable and unique gifts to receive.

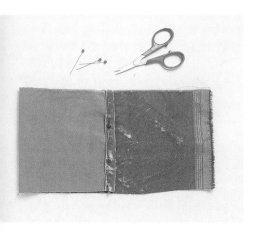
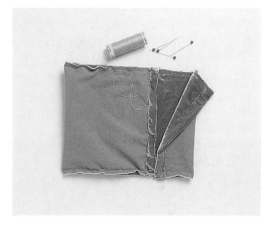

You will need

Scissors
Remnant of superb-quality
 silk velvet
Long glass-headed pins
Sewing needle and thread
Plastic heart
Metallic embroidery thread of a
 colour to match the velvet

The size and shape of your remnants of fabric may dictate the size and shape of the purse you make. Whatever size you decide upon, remember to allow for seams and a double hem since silk velvet frays badly. Another problem with this fine fabric is that it slips when machining and therefore requires pinning and basting (tacking) in place first. You may therefore find it simpler to sew by hand rather than use a sewing machine.

Collect and save unusual treasures to use for decoration, such as attractive shells, plastic "crystals", old drop earrings, tassels, sequins and beads. Ribbon or sari braid can be threaded through the tops of the purses or tied around the middle.

1. Begin by cutting a long narrow rectangle of silk velvet. Lay it on your work surface, right side uppermost, horizontally in front of you (see pictures above).

2. Take the raw edge on the left-hand short end of the rectangle and turn it under twice. Pin, then stitch in place to prevent the fabric fraying. Take this neatened end of the rectangle and fold one-third of the fabric on top of itself, right sides together, as shown. Pin in place.

3. Neaten the raw edge of the other end of the rectangle, as before, by turning it under twice and stitching. Again fold the fabric upon itself, bringing this neatened edge to meet the first one exactly.

4. Pin then stitch the two side seams together. Overstitch the raw edges of the side seams to prevent them fraying. Turn the fabric the right side out and you have a purse with a central slit for an opening. Create the purse flap by folding the top part of the purse over the bottom.

5. Stitch a plastic heart decoration on the outside of the top flap using silver metallic embroidery thread. The weight of the decoration will hold the flap in place.

RUSSET-COLOURED PURSE

You will need

Scissors
Remnant of russet-coloured
 silk velvet
Long glass-headed pins
Sewing needle and thread
Hot glue gun and glue stick
Sea shell, sprayed an antique
 gold colour

1. Cut a long narrow rectangle of silk velvet, turn in all the raw edges twice and stitch.

2. Fold one-third of the fabric on top of itself, right sides together, as for Step 2 earlier. Pin, baste (tack), then machine stitch the side seams together.

3. Turn the fabric the right side out and lay it on your work surface in front of you, the narrow rectangle stretching away from you. Fold the remaining third of fabric on top of itself, wrong sides together, bringing the top right-hand corner of this piece over to meet the bottom left-hand corner of the original rectangle, which is now positioned in the centre of the piece. Hand stitch neatly along the left-hand edge to join the pieces of fabric together.

4. Fold this top triangular part down over the bottom part of the purse to form a triangular flap. Using a hot glue gun – with the greatest of care – dab glue on the back of the decorative gold shell and stick it down on to the outside of the purse flap. (Do not apply hot glue directly on to the silk velvet.) The weight of the shell will hold the flap in place.

BROWN & SEA GREEN VELVET BAGS

The shape and style of the brown and the silver-spotted sea green bag have been dictated by the odd remnants of silk velvet.

1. Cut a long narrow rectangle of velvet about 22 x 6in (56 x 15cm). Turn both the short raw ends over twice and stitch.

2. Fold the fabric in half, right sides facing, bringing the two hemmed edges together. Pin the sides together. Measure 4in (10cm) up from the folded bottom edge of the bag and mark with a pin on both sides. Find the centre bottom of the bag and pin diagonally from this point up to the marker pins to form a sharply pointed end. Trim the excess velvet. Baste (tack) then stitch around the outside edges to make up the bag. Overstitch the raw edges to prevent fraying.

3. Turn the bag the right side out and pull into shape. Carefully push the blunt end of a pencil down into the point at the bottom of the bag. Attach a small decorative tassel or a crystal bead to the pointed end of the bag. Tie a length of sumptuous sari braid around the bag to close it.

Crackers to pull

Simple and inexpensive to make, these stylish crackers of shimmering silver on frosty white crêpe paper decorated with silver-sprayed dried cones and leaves will add the final touch to your festive table. They would also look sensational tied on the Christmas tree or entwined with a garland of fresh greenery.

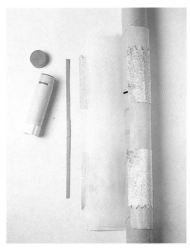

You will need (per cracker)

Pinking shears or paper edge-cutters
Two 4 x 7in (10 x 18cm) rectangles of silver crêpe paper
7 x 14in (18 x 35cm) rectangle of white crêpe paper (the longest sides cut parallel with the grain)
Stick adhesive, or hot glue gun and glue stick
6½ x 13¾in (16.5 x 34.5cm) rectangle of greaseproof paper
Cardboard tubes from kitchen paper roll
Craft knife
Cracker snap
String
Silver curling ribbon
Cracker gift, motto and hat

Natural decorations of your choice, such as tiny cones, leaves and echinops, sprayed silver (see page 16)

Have a practice run first! Once you have made one cracker, it is far easier to cut out the paper for the number of crackers you want in one go, and get into a conveyor belt system!

Cracker snaps are available from craft suppliers or good stationer's. If you don't have any cardboard tubes from kitchen paper roll or similar you could use thin card and roll it into tubes yourself.

1. Use pinking shears or paper edge-cutters to cut a neat decorative zigzag edge along one long side of each rectangle of silver crêpe paper.

2. Place your white crêpe paper rectangle on the work surface in front of you. Run a line of glue along each short side of the rectangle, about 2in (5cm) from the edge. Lay the piece of silver crêpe paper on top so that the pinked or decorated edge covers the glue, and press down to stick it to the white crêpe paper. Lift the remaining sides of the silver paper and place only a dab of glue underneath, then press down firmly.

3. Turn the crêpe paper over so that the inside of the cracker paper is uppermost. Apply two lines of glue to the greaseproof paper – parallel with the short ends of the rectangle and each line about 4in (10cm) in from the end. Centre the greaseproof paper rectangle on top of the crêpe paper; press down to stick the two sheets of paper together.

4. You will need to keep uncut two long cardboard tubes of the same diameter to help shape the paper at the ends of the crackers.

5. For the middle of the cracker, cut another cardboard tube to a length of 4¾in (12cm), using a

craft knife. Position this tube along one long edge of the white and silver rectangle, centring it so as to leave equal amounts of silver and white paper either end of it. Insert the cracker snap through the tube for the cracker and place a long tube either side of the centred cardboard tube.

6. Apply a thin line of glue along the long edge of the white and silver rectangle away from the tube. Roll up the cracker towards the glued edge and hold it in position until the paper has stuck.

7. Slightly pull out one of the longer tubes at one end of the cracker to leave a gap of 2in

(5cm) between it and the middle tube. Tie a piece of string tightly around the paper in this gap, to crimp up the paper and make the cracker shape.

8. Remove this longer tube entirely and replace the string with narrow silver ribbon.

9. Drop in through the open end of the cracker a gift and/or paper hat, motto and other bits of frivolous nonsense to add to the festive fun, before repeating Step 7 to close the other end of the cracker.

10. Stick on your chosen silver-sprayed decorations and your cracker is now finished.

Lavender bags

Handmade gifts are always extra special and these wonderfully attractive scented lavender bags are no exception. Small items of antique linen and lace, such as dressing table mats, place mats, doilies and napkins are inexpensive and are ideal for this project, as are remnants of pretty floral printed fabric.

  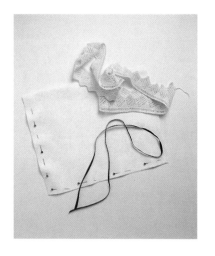 

You will need

Remnants of antique linen, lace or old fabric in lavender colours
Long glass-headed pins
Sewing machine or needle and thread
Sharp scissors
Narrow silk ribbon in deep purple, lavender and pink
Small safety pin, or large-eyed, blunt-ended needle, such as a tapestry needle
Buttons and lace edging (optional)
Loose lavender

Any of the following would be suitable for making into lavender bags: small tray cloths with lace edging; linen or broderie anglaise, square or round coaster-size mats; a damaged white damask tablecloth or large napkins from which the good fabric can be cut and used; any odd pieces of antique lace. Look, too, for children's floral clothes or old curtains at jumble sales for remnants of fabric in lavender colours. Or, if you are feeling adventurous, dye your own fabric, using a violet-coloured cold-water dye. Old linen dyes wonderfully well in the washing machine and can be sewn into lovely herb "pillows" or sachets, which can have an inside pad made from loose lavender sewn into muslin.

Loose lavender is available from shops specializing in herbs and dried flowers, aromatherapy and natural remedies, or from mail-order herbalists.

1. There are various options for differently shaped bags, depending on the shape of the fabric or the item you wish to use (see pictures above). Pin then machine or hand stitch in place. Often, little sewing is required – just a few stitches to secure the fabric into a bag of some sorts.

2. You could fold the corners of a small prettily edged square or rectangular tray cloth or mat so that they meet in the middle, to make an envelope-style bag as shown. Thread lengths of narrow ribbon decoratively through holes in the lace edging, using a small safety pin, or a large-eyed, blunt-ended needle.

3. Another option is to join together two lace doilies, coaster-size mats or similar with stitches or simply by threading ribbon through the lacy holes. Alternatively, sew plain pieces of fabric together and edge the sachet yourself by attaching a pretty lace trim.

4. Fill whatever type of bag you have made with loose lavender and seal the bag as appropriate. This could be with neat hand stitching, with a button or with ribbon threaded through and drawn tight to close the bag.

Rosebud & larch cone trees

Made from natural materials, these trees are not only delightful gifts to receive but simple to make. Old straight-sided terracotta pots are well suited to this project – look out for them on second-hand stalls.

ROSEBUD TREE

You will need

Small straight-sided terracotta
flowerpot (long Tom)
Silver-coloured gilt cream, or
matt emulsion paint in
any turquoise colour
Small paintbrush
Soft cloth (optional)
Kitchen paper
Tiny dried rosebuds
Tiny dry oasis (dry florist's foam)
ball, approx. 2in (5cm) in
diameter, plus small block of

dry oasis (dry florist's
foam)
Hot glue gun and glue stick
(optional)
Craft knife
Cinnamon stick or similar,
approx. 6in (15cm) long
Dried lichen or lavender
Ribbon

Little rosebud trees are beautiful
and fragrant. They are ideal for
a dressing table, large bathroom
or dressing room, or to scent a
guest room perhaps. Packets of

tiny rosebuds are available from
shops that specialize in herbs
and dried flowers, aromatherapy
and natural remedies, or from
mail-order herbalists, or you
could collect and dry rosebuds
from your garden, leaving a little
stem on each.

1. If the flowerpot is old, scrub
it clean and leave it to dry out
well, since terracotta is porous.

2. For a silvery pot, apply gilt
cream straight from the pot
using a paintbrush or soft cloth,

leaving patches of the terracotta
to show through. Old pots have a
rough surface and the odd crack,
and the lovely distressed finish is
easier to achieve than on a new
smooth surface.

3. To achieve the verdigris look,
apply a very small amount of
turquoise paint to the pot, using
a small paintbrush and drying the
brush on kitchen paper. Brush the
paint on in patches to give the
aged effect. Leave to dry.

4. Make a small indent in the
middle of the dry oasis ball to
denote the centre top. Push the
first rosebud into the ball here,
and work downwards in rows
(see pictures for the Larch Cone
Tree overleaf), packing the buds
closely together so that the dry
oasis cannot be seen when you
have finished. If your rosebuds
have no stems, secure them by
applying hot glue to their backs.
Leave a small gap at the base of
the ball into which to push the
cinnamon stick for the "trunk".

5. Using a craft knife, cut the
block of dry oasis into pieces
and pack them tightly inside the

painted pot. Push the cinnamon stick into the base of the rosebud ball; if it feels firm, leave it. Otherwise, withdraw the stick, apply a blob of hot glue to the end and replace it in the hole already made.

6. Repeat the process, to position the other end of the cinnamon stick in the dry oasis pieces packed into the pot.

7. Conceal the dry oasis around the base of the cinnamon stick by covering it loosely with dried lichen or lavender.

8. To complete your rosebud tree, tie a length of appropriately coloured ribbon in a bow around the cinnamon stick or around the pot as desired.

LARCH CONE TREE

You will need

Straight-sided terracotta flowerpot (long Tom), about 8in (20cm) tall
Acrylic bronze metallic paint
Small paintbrush

Dry oasis (dry florist's foam) ball, approx. 4½ in (11cm) in diameter, plus small block of dry oasis (dry florist's foam)
Larch cones
Hot glue gun and glue stick
Wooden stick and/or cinnamon stick (see below), approx. 8in (20cm) long
Secateurs
Dried lichen
Remnant of silk, metallic fabric and/or ribbon

You will require a good number of larch cones for this project, so take a big bag and go for a walk in the woods. Look for the spindly branches on the woodland floor as the tiny larch cones will still be attached, but avoid any wet black ones. I usually collect them in the autumn, but have also been successful finding them during the summer months.

For the 8in (20cm) long tree "trunk" there are several possibilities. You could use a wooden stick, cut from a straight section of a small branch of hazel, willow or ash; cut a thick short cane to size or bind

together three or four thin cinnamon sticks or use one substantial one.

In place of the dried lichen used to cover the dry oasis at the base of the "trunk" you could use star anise (an exotic dried seed pod), small nuts, Christmassy pot-pourri, or colourful acrylic "jewels", which pick up the colour of the remnant of fabric or ribbon tied around the pot.

1. Prepare your flowerpot as before then paint it with the bronze paint and leave to dry.

2. Make the cone ball in the same way as the rose ball. Push the first cone into what will be the centre top of the ball, applying hot glue to its stem to hold it securely. Continue by working in a line down the ball. In the same way, quarter the ball vertically with larch cones to divide it into four equal sections to work on. It is essential to pack the cones close together so that the dry oasis cannot be seen when you have finished. Fill in any gaps. You may find it easier to rest the ball on another flowerpot while you work.

4. Leave a small gap at the base of the cone-covered ball, just large enough to push in a wooden stick so as to make a hole for the "trunk". Remove the stick and apply hot glue to its end or to the end of the cinnamon stick – whichever you are using – before placing it in the hole in the dry oasis ball.

5. Using a craft knife, cut the block of dry oasis into pieces and pack them tightly inside the bronzed pot. Again, use the wooden stick to make a hole in the dry oasis in the pot. Remove the stick and hot glue the "trunk" in place, ensuring that it is centred and completely vertical.

6. Conceal the dry oasis around the base of the "trunk" by covering it loosely with lichen or other material of your choice.

7. To complete the tree, wrap a length of colourful fabric and/or ribbon around the pot and tie it in an extravagant bow.

Painted glassware

Glass painting is simple, quick and fun to do. You need not be an artist – even circles, squiggles and blobs outlined in silver or gold look amazingly effective. Glass is available everywhere, both new and secondhand. Hunt around for pretty pieces to decorate for Christmas presents – have a go and you'll find yourself hooked!

SMARTENED BUBBLE BATH BOTTLES

You will need

Recycled glass bottles
Gold or silver relief outliner (contour paste)
No. 4 artist's paintbrush
Water-based glass paints in solid, vibrant colours (see page 106)
Artist's concentrated liquid colours in opalescent colours nearest to the colours of the glass paints you are using, e.g. opalescent violet over purple or violet, opalescent white over anything, opalescent green over green, etc.
Two-part epoxy glue
Glass nuggets or similar decorations (optional)

These glass bottles previously held bubble bath; their large flat surfaces make them perfect for decorating. You can then decant another bath product into each one to use all over again or use them as candle holders over the festive season. Here, the main shapes were outlined with relief outliner and then filled in with water-based paints – a bit like a stained-glass effect.

1. Carefully wash the bottles well to remove any greasy fingermarks and dust and leave to dry.

2. Using the gold or silver outliner, draw the basic shape of the design on the bottles and leave to dry for about 1 hour.

3. Using a no. 4 artist's paintbrush, fill in the design with the solid-coloured water-based glass paints and leave to dry for at least 1 hour.

4. Overpaint the design with the opalescent liquid colours if you wish and leave to dry.

5. Prepare the epoxy glue according to the manufacturer's instructions and use it to stick glass nuggets or other appropriate decorations on the bottles, if liked, once the paint is completely dry.

VIBRANT VOTIVE CANDLE HOLDERS

You will need

Glass candle holders
Gold relief outliner (contour paste)
Royal blue water- or solvent-based glass paint (see page 106)
No. 3 artist's paintbrush

These small tumbler-like glass pots are made from thick, weighty glass, specifically made for candles; however, any small tumblers or tot glasses will suffice. This is very simple and therefore ideal for your first glass painting project. Use plain, vibrant or seasonal colours in simple designs.

1. Carefully wash the candle holders to remove greasy finger-marks and dust and leave to dry.

2. Decorate the glass with spirals of gold and blue and with a band of colour around the top edge. It is entirely a matter of preference whether you use the gold outliner first – direct from the tube – and then apply the blue glass paint, or the other way around.

Do whichever you find the easiest, leaving the first colour to dry thoroughly before proceeding with the second. The outliner will take about 1 hour to dry, as will water-based glass paint, while solvent-based glass paint should be left overnight to dry.

3. Once the paint is completely dry, place candles inside the glasses ready for use.

BLUE FLOWER BOTTLES

You will need

Glass bottles and/or tumblers
No. 3 artist's paintbrush
Solvent-based glass paints (such as Vitrail) in blue, yellow and green (see page 106)
Appropriate thinner or white spirit
Kitchen paper
Silver relief outliner (contour paste)

Here you can create your own unique range of glassware. The sparkling clarity of deep blue flowers with yellow centres, painted in simple childlike shapes, enhance prettily shaped bottles and tumblers. As with the votive candle holders earlier, it is a matter of preference whether you "draw" them first with a fine outliner and fill them in with paint, or paint first and outline them once the paint is dry. Have fun creating your own designs in the colours of your choice. Once you start painting glass, you will not be able to stop!

1. Carefully wash the glassware well to remove greasy finger-marks and dust and leave to dry.

2. Using a no. 3 paintbrush and blue glass paint, paint daisy-like flower heads on the prepared glass. Leave to dry for about 1 hour. Rinse the brush in the appropriate thinner or white spirit and dry it on kitchen paper.

3. Using the cleaned paintbrush, fill in the flower centres with yellow paint. Rinse the brush as

before and, when the yellow paint is touch dry after about 1 hour, paint green stems beneath the flowers if liked.

4. When the paint is touch dry, outline the flowers with silver relief outliner, or leave plain. Leave overnight to dry thoroughly.

JEWEL COLOURS ON GILDED WINE GLASSES

You will need

Inexpensive wine glasses
No. 8 artist's paintbrush
Water-based glass paints in violet and pink (see page 106)
Small paintbrush
Acrylic gold size
2–3 sheets of Dutch metal transfer leaf

Soft brush
Gold relief outliner (contour paste) (optional)

These richly gilded glasses in jewel colours will be something for your guests to feast their eyes on over Christmas. You should not eat or drink directly off glass-painted surfaces, so regard these glasses as purely decorative objects, or fill them with whole nuts or foil-wrapped chocolates. They cannot be dishwashed, and require careful washing in cold water.

1. Carefully wash the wine glasses well to remove greasy fingermarks and dust and leave to dry.

2. Using the no. 8 artist's paintbrush, paint the outside of the wine glasses all over with violet

or pink water-based glass paint. Leave to dry for about 1 hour.

3. For a more intense colour apply a second coat of paint, but only do so when the first coat is absolutely dry otherwise it will remove the paint. Leave to dry.

4. Using a small paintbrush, brush the acrylic gold size on to the areas of the wine glasses to be gilded, i.e. the rims and stems

of the wine glasses. Leave for at least 15 minutes until the gold size is tacky.

5. Cut the transfer leaf into strips and gently press it on to the gold-sized areas, smoothing your fingers over the sheet until all of the leaf has transferred to the surface of the pots. Remove the backing tissue. Use a soft brush gently over the gilded areas to remove any excess Dutch metal leaf.

6. Decorate the glasses further using gold relief outliner, if liked, drawing patterns such as the bows shown here.

GLASS PAINTS & RELIEF OUTLINER

Glass paints come in a vast range of brilliant colours, which will enhance the most ordinary pieces. There are two mediums – water-based and solvent-based – and both are excellent. Use either water- or solvent-based glass paints for one project – do not mix the two mediums. Solvent-based paints flow extremely well; they have good lightfastness and the transparent colour shades are intermixable – black and white are opaque. All are touch dry in about 1 hour but should be left overnight to dry completely. Brushes should be cleaned in white spirit or Vitrail thinner. Water-based paints dry more

quickly, taking about 1 hour to dry. Glass paints are generally for decorative purposes and painted glassware will resist only light washing in cold water.

Before using relief outliner, unscrew the cap from the tube and pierce the nozzle with a pin to ensure a fine line of paste will be released. (Piercing the tube with anything larger than a pin will make it impossible to draw a fine line, or to control the flow of colour.) To use the outliner, place the tip lightly on the surface of the glass and squeeze gently and evenly while pulling the tube along the surface. Wipe away any mistakes immediately with a cotton bud.

OCTAGONAL GLASSES

You will need

Octagonal wine glasses
Nos. 5 and 2 artist's
*   paintbrushes*
Solvent-based glass paints
*   (such as Vitrail) in warm*
*   green and blue (see below)*
Appropriate thinner or white
*   spirit*
Kitchen paper
Silver and gold fine relief
*   outliners (contour paste)*
Water-based glass paints in
*   violet and pink*

These pretty little octagonal wine glasses were a bargain from a local charity shop. The blue and green ones are painted in solvent-based glass paints, which take longer to dry but the colours are beautifully intense.

As before, you should not drink from glass-painted surfaces, so regard these glasses as purely decorative objects. They cannot be dishwashed, and need careful washing in cold water.

1. Carefully wash and dry the wine glasses as before.

2. For the green glass, leave two opposite facets of the octagon unpainted. Using a no. 5 paint-brush for the main parts of the glass and the finer no. 2 brush for the more fiddly areas, paint the other six sides down to the bottom, leaving the underneath clear. Paint the stem and the base in solid green. Leave to dry for at least 1 hour. Rinse the brush in the appropriate thinner or white spirit and dry it on kitchen paper.

3. Using the silver relief outliner, highlight the vertical angled edges on the glass. Fill in between these with a triangular or zigzag pattern which should match up all the way around the glass. Make a criss-cross pattern down the stem and a simple leaf design on the base.

4. If you wish, use the silver relief outliner to paint a delicate leaf pattern in the sections of

clear unpainted glass. Once the outliner is dry, use the very tip of a no. 5 paintbrush to fill in the leaves with a little green glass paint. Leave to dry overnight.

5. For the blue glass, paint the top part of the glass as far as the top of the stem, applying the blue paint with a cleaned no. 5 brush. Then paint a narrow band of blue twisting around the clear glass stem down to the base. Paint the base blue and leave to dry for at least 1 hour.

6. As before, highlight the vertical angled edges of the glass with silver outliner, this time continuing the lines as far as the top of the stem. Decorate between these lines with a simple webbing pattern, and use a fish-scale effect around alternate bottom sections. Leave overnight to dry thoroughly.

7. For the pink and violet octagonal glasses pictured, use the water-based paints of the gilded wine glass project on page 105. Leaving two opposite facets unpainted, paint the top and the base of the glasses with a solid colour and paint a twisting band of colour around the stem as for the blue glass above. Use gold outliner to highlight the vertical angled edges as far as the top of the stem. Decorate the two clear glass sections and the base of each glass with a fish-scale effect of gold. Leave to dry overnight.

Same-day sensations

Although these projects take a little longer to make they are well worth it. Velvet features in sumptuous crackers and some unusual Christmas tree decorations, while tinware is given an attractive paint finish to make very acceptable gifts for men and tin is the basis for the Mexican-style decorations. The painted hatboxes are glamorous and the silk-covered boxes will appeal to those who like sewing.

Velvet tree decorations

Although these lovely velvet-covered and bejewelled tree decorations look very expensive, two were made from the polystyrene trays used in shops for packaging pears! The others are made from polystyrene shapes purchased from craft suppliers. They are covered in remnants of silk velvet and braid.

2. Starting at the top of the polystyrene ball, draw lines downwards to divide the ball into four segments, then draw a line around the middle of the ball to create a total of eight sections.

3. Using these marks as a guide, pin a small piece of velvet over one of the sections and draw the section outline on to the fabric. If the material is too dark for the outline to show up, simply trim the fabric back to within ⅛in (3mm) of the section shape all around.

4. Using this piece as a template, cut out a total of eight pieces of velvet. Working with one section at a time, apply hot or fabric glue to the polystyrene ball within the lines drawn. Stick a section of velvet in place. Attach all the remaining pieces of velvet in the same way, overlapping the edges of each piece slightly until the ball is completely covered with pieces of velvet.

5. Trim any untidy bits of velvet and glue a length of braid horizontally around the middle of the bauble to cover the raw edges of the velvet sections.

BALL-SHAPED BAUBLES

You will need

Polystyrene balls
Ballpoint or felt-tip pen
Long glass-headed pins
Remnants of velvet or any
 soft fabric
Scissors
Hot glue gun and glue stick,
 or a fast fabric glue
Remnants of braid
Length of silk cord, or tasselled cord
 from a small tie-back

Sewing needle and thread
Decorations such as acrylic
 jewels, faceted beads,
 sheesha mirror glass,
 sequins

There are many items suitable for decorating these luxurious-looking baubles – look in bead or general craft suppliers for a variety of beads, faceted and smooth acrylic or glass flat-backed "jewels" (decorative stones), rhinestone crystals,

sequins and spangles. Sheesha glass is another option. This is the tiny pieces of roughly cut mirror glass, commonly used in Indian embroidery. The pieces come in several shapes and sizes and are available from shops selling Indian silks and fabrics, from good embroidery/craft shops and from large craft suppliers.

1. Take a polystyrene ball and mark what is to be the top of the bauble clearly with a ballpoint or felt-tip pen.

6. Take a length of cord, and allowing extra for the loop at the top of the bauble, stick the cord over the vertical raw edges of the velvet. Secure the cord to the polystyrene ball with long pins, which wil help hold it in place until the glue dries sufficiently.

7. Sew all the cords together neatly at the top of the bauble and form a loop by which to hang the bauble. If using tasselled cord, such as a small tie-back, allow the tassel to hang beneath the bauble.

8. Finally, taking great care, glue on to the velvet bauble any acrylic or glass jewels, beads, sheesha glass or similar decorations, applying glue to their backs and pressing them firmly on to the velvet.

HEART-SHAPED BAUBLES

You will need

*Remnant of velvet or any
    soft fabric*
Polystyrene hearts
Long glass-headed pins
Scissors
*Hot glue gun and glue stick,
    or a fast fabric glue*
Length of silk cord
Sewing needle and thread
*Plastic or glass chandelier-style
    "crystals" or other suitable
    hanging decoration*

1. Hold a piece of velvet over one side of a polystyrene heart, using the fabric on the bias so that it can be pulled taut. Pin it in position, making the necessary adjustments until it fits, then cut out the shape, allowing an extra 1/8in (3mm) of fabric all round to overlap or trim as necessary.

2. Using this as a template, cut out two velvet shapes per heart. Glue each piece on separately to cover the shape, overlapping the edges of the fabric slightly to cover the polystyrene. Trim any untidy bits.

3. Allowing for sufficient cord to make a loop at the top by which to suspend the bauble, and using the cord either singly or doubled to cover the messy edges at the sides of the heart, measure and cut the cord to length. Glue it in position, securing it with pins until securely stuck.

4. As before, secure the cords at the top of the bauble with neat stitching and form the loop. Sew chandelier-style crystals to the base of the bauble.

PEAR-SHAPED BAUBLES

You will need

Polystyrene pear tray
Craft knife
*Remnants of velvet or any
    soft fabric*
Scissors
Long glass-headed pins
*Hot glue gun and glue stick,
    or a fast fabric glue*
Sewing needle and thread
String
Remnants of braid
*Decorations such as acrylic
    jewels, faceted beads,
    coiled gold thread*

1. If using a polystyrene pear tray, cut out the half pear shapes, using a craft knife. Place two together and trim until they fit snugly to make a whole "pear".

2. You may find it easier to cover each polystyrene half separately

with fabric and then join them together. To do this, wrap a piece of velvet over each pear half and cut out the shape roughly. Then stretch the velvet over each shape, pin and glue down, turning the raw edges of the fabric over the edge of the shape slightly. This gives two neatly covered pear halves which can be sewn together with small neat stitches. Tie string around them first if you find this easier.

3. The alternative is to glue the two polystyrene halves together and tie with string to hold them firm until the glue dries. Then cover the whole shape with two pieces of fabric as you did for the heart shape.

4. Whichever method you choose to cover the pear shape, you will probably want to stick braid around it to mask where the two halves meet and to use extra as the loop by which to

hang the bauble. As before, glue the braid in place and secure with long pins while the glue dries.

5. Finish by sticking on small acrylic jewels or similar decorations as before, applying the glue to their backs and pressing them firmly on to the velvet bauble. Another decorative touch is to take fine gold wire thread, wind it into a coil shape and secure it to the velvet with a few fine stitches.

PLAIN RED VELVET DECORATION

You will need

Remnants of velvet or any soft fabric
Small polystyrene ball
Long glass-headed pins
Scissors
Hot glue gun and glue stick, or a fast fabric glue

Sewing needle and thread
Gold wire thread (optional)
Remnants of braid
Decorations such as leaf-shaped cake decorations, chandelier-style crystals, acrylic jewels and sequins

1. To make the plain dark red velvet decoration, stretch a piece of velvet over the bottom half of a small polystyrene ball using it on the bias as you did in Step 1 of the heart-shaped bauble.

2. Pin then cut the piece of velvet to fit. Glue it in position on the bottom half of the ball and trim the raw edges.

3. The top half of the decoration is like a little bag. To make this, cut out a small rectangle of the same coloured velvet. With right sides together pin then stitch the two short ends of the rectangle together to make a tube shape.

4. Turn the fabric the right side out and turn under the raw edge along the bottom of the "tube". Glue this neatened edge around the middle of the polystyrene ball, butting it up to the velvet already glued in place. Hold with pins until firmly stuck.

5. Gather the velvet at the top of the "tube", turn in the raw edges and sew the "bag" closed. An alternative and quicker option is to simply tie gold wire thread tightly around the top of the fabric, knot it and make the excess into a loop by which to hang the bauble.

6. Attach two leaf-shaped cake decorations to the top of the bauble and stitch chandelier-style crystals to the bottom. Decorate the bauble further by glueing jewels or sequins in place, as before.

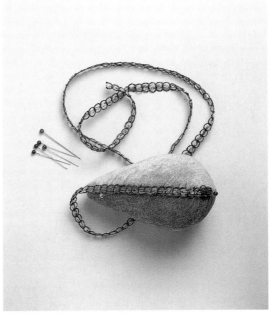

Painted hatboxes

These decorated hatboxes make fabulous Christmas presents! The options are endless – hatboxes painted in sizzling colours and adorned with shot-silk ribbon tied in a large floppy bow, with Indian sari braid or edged with rope trimming, with the additions of scattered sequins and silk or paper flowers. The effects are sensational.

1. Paint the hatbox and lid, inside and out, as well as underneath, with at least two coats of matt emulsion paint, allowing the paint to dry between coats. Leave to dry thoroughly.

2. Replace the lid on the hatbox. Using the glitter glue, decorate the top and the side of the box with scrolls, squiggles or any other all-over design. Take care not to touch the glitter glue as it takes 1–2 hours to dry completely, and will smudge and be difficult to remove.

3. Apply tiny blobs of hot glue at intervals around the edge of the lid and stick the gold sequins on top, taking great care not to burn your fingers. Leave to dry.

4. Pass the wire-edged ribbon underneath the box and tie on top in a flamboyant bow. Trim the loose ends by folding the very end of each lengthways in half and cutting across at an angle to make a perfectly symmetrical inverted "V" in each ribbon tail.

5. Stick an attractive paper or silk flower and gold foil leaf-shaped cake decorations on top of the lid for extra effect.

FUCHSIA PINK HATBOX

You will need

Sturdy card/papier mâché round hatbox, 12in (30cm) in diameter and 6½in (16.5cm) tall
1in (2.5cm) household paintbrush
Matt emulsion paint in vibrant pink or red
High-tack gold glitter glue with fine applicator nozzle
Hot glue gun and glue stick
Heart-shaped gold sequins
Pink, wide wire-edged shot-silk ribbon
Scissors
Paper or silk flower
Gold foil leaf-shaped cake decorations

PURPLE HATBOX

You will need

Sturdy card/papier mâché round hatbox, 12in (30cm) in diameter and 6½in (16.5cm) tall
1in (2.5cm) household paintbrush
Matt emulsion paint in purple
1 yd (1 m) wide sari braid
Scissors
2 long glass-headed pins
Pencil
Fabric glue, or hot glue gun and glue stick
Clothes pegs

1. Paint the hatbox and lid, inside and out, as well as underneath, with at least two coats of purple matt emulsion paint, allowing the paint to dry between coats. Leave to dry thoroughly.

2. Wrap the sari braid around the box to estimate how much to cut. Allow extra braid for a small overlap and for both raw ends to be turned under. Cut the braid to length, turn under the raw ends and wrap around the box again. At the point where the braid

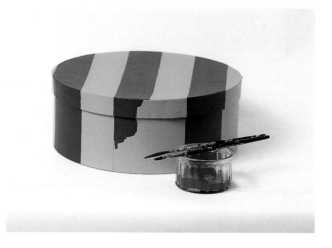

overlaps slightly, secure it with pins. Ensure the braid is centred all the way around the box and perfectly flat, before making a faint pencil mark if necessary as a guide.

3. Remove the pins and braid from the box once more. Take one end of the braid with its turned under raw edge and glue into position on the box. Working around the box, stick the rest of the length of braid in place and glue down the final turned-under raw end.

4. To finish the lid, cut the braid to a length to run as a band across the lid, allowing for both raw ends to be turned under. Turn the lid upside down and run a line of glue the width of the ribbon on the inside edge. Turn under one end of the length of braid and press the folded end firmly to the glue. Take the braid across the lid to the opposite side. Turn under the raw end and glue firmly inside the lid as before. Hold the braid in place with clothes pegs until the glue dries. Use more braid to make an attractive bow. Trim the raw ends

evenly, fold them under for a neater look and stitch or glue to avoid fraying. Stick the bow on top of the band of braid.

5. Alternatively, cut two long lengths of braid and turn under one end of each length to stop fraying. Position these turned under ends on opposite sides of the lid and glue to the inside edge of the lid as before. Hold in place with clothes pegs until the glue dries. Finally, tie the loose ends of the braid into a large, flat bow on top of the lid. Neaten the raw ends as before.

STRIPED HATBOX

You will need

Sturdy card/papier mâché round hatbox, 12in (30cm) in diameter and 4in (10cm) tall
1in (2.5cm) household paintbrush
Matt emulsion paint in pale lime green and blue
Pencil
Ruler
Lining brush (optional)

No. 8 artist's paintbrush
Scissors
Wide wire-edged ribbon
Fabric glue and/or hot glue gun and glue stick
Clothes pegs or long glass-headed pins
Decorative cord
Gold filigree ribbon
Sheets of pink tissue paper, for the tissue paper flowers (optional)
Drinking glass or egg cup

Check whether your hatbox has a particularly tight-fitting lid, as the fit does vary and it will affect how you decorate this box. Recheck after the box has been painted when the paint is dry, to determine how you will attach the ribbon to the sides of the box (see Steps 3–6). You will need more patience and a steady hand for this hatbox.

1. Paint the hatbox and lid, inside and out, as well as underneath, with at least two coats of the green matt emulsion, allowing the paint to dry between coats. Apply a third coat if necessary for a good strong colour. Leave the paint to dry.

2. With the lid in place and using a pencil and ruler, mark out the stripes on the box, shading the area to be painted blue. The simplest way is to determine the middle of the lid using the ruler, decide upon the width of the stripes and position the first one in the centre. Continue marking out the stripes, measuring outwards from the central one. Continue the stripes down the sides of the lid and the box.

3. If the lid of your hatbox is tight fitting, have the lid in place and make horizontal pencil marks where the lid meets the top of the stripes – these need to remain visible even after you paint in the blue. This is where the top of the ribbon on the side of the hatbox will begin – otherwise the lid will not fit on the box. If the lid is a loose fitting one, however, as in the main picture, the ribbon (and painted) stripes can run right to the top edge of the box.

4. You will find it easier to have the lid in place for painting the blue stripes so that you can paint each stripe in a more or less

continuous line. If using a lining brush, it is probably easiest if you have the box on a flat work surface and stand up and lean over it. Dip the liner in the blue emulsion paint, and use it to outline the edges of each stripe. Steady your hand by resting your little finger against the box, taking care not to smudge the paint as you work. Pull the lining brush towards you, replenishing the paint when necessary, and carefully replacing the tip of the liner where you broke off the colour.

5. Fill in the main body of the outlined blue stripes on the box and the lid, using the no. 8 artist's paintbrush. The blue stripes will require two or three coats of paint to eradicate the brush marks (by the time you have touched up the stripes here and there, it is simpler to go over the whole stripe again to even out the colour). Do not worry too much if you make a mistake as you can cover one or both sides of every blue stripe with ribbon if you wish. (If your box lid is loose enough and your ribbon stripes are going to run right to the top

edge of the box, you might prefer to remove the lid and continue the blue painted stripes to the top, too.) Leave the paint to dry.

6. Cut the ribbon into equal lengths for the side of the box – either to run right to the top edge of the box, or to end at the pencil marks where the lid begins. Measure the required height of ribbon from the bottom of the box, allowing for turning under the raw ends of ribbon, plus an extra 1in (2.5cm) to tuck under the base of the box. Glue the lengths of ribbon in place to one or both sides of every blue stripe, using fabric or hot glue. If using fabric glue, hold the ribbon ends in place with clothes pegs on the top edge of the box, or push pins into the box to hold the shorter lengths temporarily while the glue dries.

7. Replace the lid and line up the painted stripes on the lid with those on the box. Before cutting the ribbon for the stripes on the lid, which run from the outside edge on one side of the lid to the edge on the far side, measure each one in turn since these will

vary in length. As before, allow a little extra on each length of ribbon – about $\frac{3}{8}$–$\frac{1}{2}$in (1–1.5cm) – for turning under the raw ends on the edge of the lid. Glue the ribbon in place.

8. Glue the decorative cord around the side of the lid along the top edge, making sure to overlap the ends of the cord and glue them together neatly since cord unravels easily.

9. Cut the gold filigree ribbon for the decorative "handle", allowing a little extra at each end – about $\frac{3}{4}$in (2cm) – to attach each end to the inside of the box lid. Glue in place. If the lid is too tight fitting to allow this, simply turn the raw ends of ribbon under and stick on the outside of the lid.

FOR THE TISSUE PAPER FLOWERS

10. To make a decorative paper flower, fold a sheet of pink tissue paper several times until you have a square of about $3\frac{1}{2}$–4in (9–10cm), which is many layers thick. Draw around an upturned

glass or other circular object on the paper. Cut through all the layers to produce many circles.

11. Build up the flower in layers of petals, rather like a rose, using several of the tissue circles for the base of the flower head, some folded in half or quarters and others pinched-in at the base. Glue all the tissue circles together in the centre with a tiny spot of hot glue, making the flower look as realistic as possible. Take care not to let the glue dribble as the tissue will tear and make a mess.

12. For the centre of the flower, cut or tear another piece of tissue paper into a strip about 2 x 9in (5 x 23cm) and fold the raw edges towards the middle. Twist the strip of paper around in a closely wound circle or knot to resemble the centre of a rose. Hot glue at the back to secure, then stick into the centre of the almost completed flower.

13. Make two or three paper flowers to decorate the lid of the hatbox and stick in place.

Mexican-style embossed tin decorations

Embossed metal is an ancient craft currently enjoying a popular revival. It has many possibilities – ranging from small decorative items to tabletops, furniture panels and inlays. The sheets of metallic foil come in silver, brass and copper colours and, although not easy to find, are well worth tracking down.

You will need

White drawing paper
Pencil
Ruler
Small scissors
Embossing metallic foils in gold, copper, silver and blue
Cardboard or self-healing stencil mat for a cutting base
Ballpoint pen, hard pencil or fine knitting needle
Fine scalpel
Two-part epoxy glue
Solvent-based glass paints (such as Vitrail) in carmine, yellow, turquoise and violet (see page 106)
Fine artist's paintbrush
Appropriate thinner or white spirit
Kitchen paper
Narrow ribbon
Fine sewing needle

You don't have to stick to the heart and star shapes given here. You can follow the instructions below to make any other shape of tin decoration that you like, for example, crowns, angels or geometric shapes. To give any of these tin decorations extra strength, so that they are less bendy, cut out and decorate a duplicate shape and stick the two pieces back to back to give a stronger, double-sided decoration.

HEART TEMPLATE

HEART

1. To achieve a symmetrical shape, fold a piece of white drawing paper in half. Using a pencil, draw the outline of half a heart, measuring approximately 1¼in (3cm) at the widest part, so that the heart is about 2½in (6.5cm) across when opened out. In the same way, cut out a smaller version, measuring about 1in (2.5cm) at the widest part when opened out. Alternatively, use the templates provided and adapt them to the size of decoration you require.

2. Place a sheet of gold foil on your cutting base and place the larger paper pattern on top. Carefully draw around the shape using a ballpoint pen, hard pencil, knitting needle or similar blunt-ended tool, adding a loop or link shape at the top of the heart by which to hang the decoration on the tree.

3. Remove the paper template and carefully cut out the foil

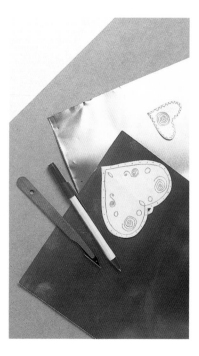

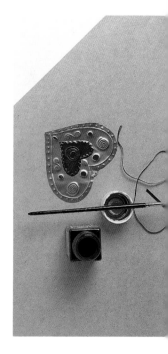

heart using scissors. Use a fine scalpel to remove the centre of the loop.

4. Cut the smaller heart from copper foil in the same manner. Place the small heart on top of the larger one so as to give yourself an idea of the area to be decorated with embossing. Plan your embossed design on the paper templates if liked before you begin.

5. Start with the larger heart and decide which side of the foil will be the "wrong" side. With this side uppermost, use your blunt-ended tool to press and "draw" the design into the foil. "Draw" a line around the inside edge of the heart. Next, impress a line of dots around the edge, then circles, an

oval and spirals in the area that will lie between the heart shapes.

6. Take the smaller heart and again decide which will be the reverse side. Impress a pattern on it by "drawing" a zigzag design around the edge and a spiral in the centre.

7. Turn both hearts over so that their raised patterns are uppermost. Prepare the epoxy glue according to the manufacturer's instructions. Apply glue to the reverse of the smaller heart and press it on to the front of the larger one. Leave the glue to harden for about 30 minutes before painting.

8. Decorate the hearts with glass paints, using a fine paintbrush;

always rinse the brush in thinner or white spirit and dry it on kitchen paper before moving on to the next colour. Use carmine-coloured paint on the larger heart for the circles and oval, and yellow on the outer edge.

9. Leave the paint to dry overnight then thread a length of narrow ribbon through the loop at the top of the heart ready for hanging. If the foil decoration needs flattening, leave the painted heart overnight once more – this time pressed between the pages of a heavy book, weighted down with more books piled on top.

FOUR-POINTED STAR

1. As you did for the heart decoration, begin by making paper patterns of two four-pointed stars. One should be about 4in (10cm) across, and the other roughly half the size – about 2in (5cm) across. Either fold a piece of drawing paper in half and draw the outline of half a star each time, which will be opened out to give a symmetrical star, or trace around the star templates provided using pencil and paper and adapt them to the size of decoration you require.

2. Place a sheet of silver metallic foil on your cutting base. Place the larger paper star on top and carefully draw around

the template with a blunt-ended tool as before. Remove the paper template and cut out the foil star using scissors. Set aside.

3. Cut the smaller star from blue foil in the same manner. As before, plan your design on the paper templates if liked, before you begin embossing.

4. Take the large silver foil star and use your blunt-ended tool to "draw" and press the design into the "wrong" side of the foil, as before. Draw a line around the inside edge of the star; impress diamond shapes into the points of the star then rub over the diamond shapes to raise the design. Impress lines of dots in the corner points of the star.

5. Take the smaller foil star and again "draw" a line around the inside edge of the "wrong" side of the foil. Impress a series of oval shapes in the foil, one in the centre of the star, and the other four in the centre of the four radiating points.

6. Turn both stars over so that their raised patterns are uppermost. Prepare the epoxy glue according to the manufacturer's instructions. Apply glue to the reverse of the smaller star and press it on to the front of the larger one. Leave the glue to harden for about 30 minutes before painting the star decoration.

7. Decorate the stars with glass paints as before. Paint a diamond shape in each point with the turquoise-coloured glass paint. Paint the blue star with the remaining glass paints.

8. Pierce a hole in the top of the star with a fine needle through which to thread narrow ribbon for hanging it up. Leave the paint to dry overnight and complete as for the heart shape.

STAR TEMPLATE

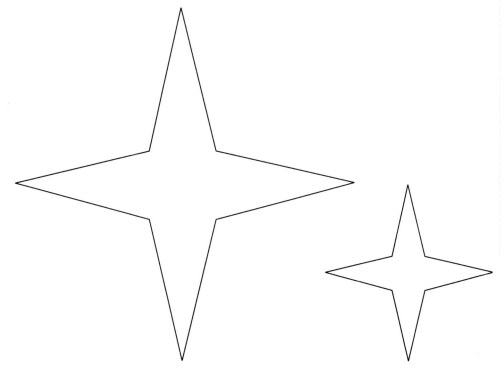

Snowy velvet crackers

These lovely crackers are for effect and are not to be pulled! They look particularly attractive displayed on a white damask cloth with other white festive decorations. They also look stunning against the dark green of a real Christmas tree.

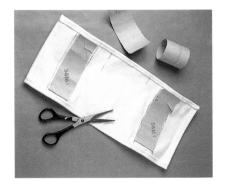  

You will need (per cracker)

16 x 8in (40 x 20cm) rectangle of white velvet
Tape measure or ruler
Long glass-headed pins
Sewing machine or needle and white thread
Scissors
Cardboard tubes from 2 toilet rolls
Ballpoint pen
Hot glue gun and glue stick
Two 8in (20cm) lengths of string
Wide, wire-edged sheer white ribbon

A ½ yd (0.5m) remnant of white velvet is ample for six crackers.

1. To neaten the raw edges of the fabric, turn under ½in (1.5cm) on the shorter sides of the rectangle of velvet and secure with pins. Repeat on the longer sides. Machine or hand stitch in place.

2. Cut one of the cardboard tubes in half to make two shorter tubes. Cut these two half-tubes so as to open them up.

3. Lay the velvet in front of you, wrong side uppermost. Using a tape measure and ballpoint pen, find and mark the centre of one long side of the fabric rectangle.

4. Lay the longer uncut cardboard tube on the wrong side of the fabric, against the long marked side, and centre it over the mark on the fabric. Using the pen, make marks on the fabric at either end of the cardboard tube.

5. Measure 1½in (4cm) away from the ends of the tube and make more marks – the space between these marks represents the gap between the tubes where the cracker will be pinched in and tied with ribbon.

6. Measure and mark two more points, another 2in (5cm) from the last lines.

7. Open out the cut half-tubes. Apply hot glue to the velvet between the last set of marks at each end of the rectangle, which are 2in (5cm) apart. Flatten out the tubes in these spaces.

8. Apply glue to the end pieces of velvet, beyond the cardboard, and fold these inwards, sticking them down on to the cardboard.

9. Run a line of glue along the edge of the velvet between the pen marks for the centre cardboard tube. Hold the tube in place for a moment until stuck.

10. Roll the centre tube across the velvet, making sure the fabric is straight and pulling taut. When everything is aligned, run a line

of hot glue along the machined edge of the velvet for the length of the tube. Hold firmly in position until the glue adheres.

11. Repeat the rolling and gluing of the end tubes – you may have to push your fingers inside the ends of the cracker to press down the fabric being glued – take care not to burn your fingers.

12. Tie a length of string around one end of the cracker in the gap between the lengths of tube and pull tight to draw the cracker into a good shape. Cut an extra long length of wire-edged sheer ribbon to tie in a bow, removing the string as you tighten the ribbon. Once the bow is tied, bend the ends into more loops in an extravagant fashion. Complete the cracker by tying the other end, first with string then with ribbon, in the same way.

Silk-covered boxes

Combine remnants of jewel-bright silks with beads, sequins and braids to create these beautiful giftboxes. Such card or papier mâché boxes are available from craft suppliers in many shapes and sizes, and leftover padded curtain interlining works perfectly beneath the silk.

ORANGE TREASURE CHEST

You will need

Sturdy card/papier mâché domed
    treasure-chest box
Small paintbrush
Matt emulsion paint in an orange
    to match the silk
Sharp scissors
Padded curtain interlining
Tape measure
Fabric glue
Vibrant orange pure silk
Iron
Long glass-headed pins
Sewing machine or needle
    and thread
Braid
Old clasp or drop earring

1. Paint the box inside and out all over, using a small paintbrush and orange matt emulsion paint. Allow the first coat to dry before applying a second coat of paint. Leave to dry.

2. Next, cut out the interlining for the box. Since it will be concealed beneath the silk and it does not fray, there is no need to allow extra interlining for turning the raw edges. Stand one end of the box on the interlining to mark out the domed piece required for each end of the box. Cut across these two pieces to allow for when the lid is open. Trim each piece back a little from this last cut so that when in place the

interlining falls a little short of the opening edge of the box.

3. Next, cut a long rectangular piece of interlining to wrap around the box, running from about ½in (1.5cm) short of the front opening edge of the box, underneath the box, up the back and over the lid on top of the box to end about ½in (1.5cm) short of the lid opening edge.

4. Glue the pieces of interlining to the surface of the box with fabric glue.

5. Cut similar pieces of silk – a rectangle to wrap around the box and the end pieces – this time

allowing for an extra good ½in (1.5cm) on each edge for turning under the raw edges and for the seams. Press all the pieces of silk.

6. Neatly hem the short ends of the large silk rectangle by turning under twice the extra ½in (1.5cm) of fabric allowed for at each end. Pin, then machine or hand stitch.

7. In the same way, on each of the four end pieces hem the raw edge that will align with the opening edges of the box.

8. Wrap the hemmed rectangle of silk around the box, wrong side uppermost, centring the box within the fabric. The hemmed

additional lengths on the top edges of the lid, always turning under the raw ends of braid. To complete the box, attach an old clasp, pretty button or drop earring to the lid for decoration.

SEA GREEN HATBOX

You will need

Sturdy card/papier mâché round hatbox, 11in (27.5cm) in diameter and 6½in (16.5cm) tall

Matt emulsion paint in a green to match the silk

Small paintbrush

Tape measure

Sea green silk dupion

Pencil

Scissors

Iron

Clothes pegs or small bulldog clips

Hot glue gun and glue stick

Long glass-headed pins

Sewing machine or needle and thread

Fabric glue

Wide, wire-edged ribbon

Gold sequins

It is entirely up to you whether you want to paint this hatbox inside, or line it with silk glued in place, as here. The other difference with this project is that interlining is not used here and the silk used is dupion, which is much easier to work with since it does not fray as much.

This project is possible only if the lid of your box is not too close-fitting, otherwise the lid will not fit over the silk-covered side of the box.

ends should align with the front edges of the box and lid. Push pins through the silk into the interlining to hold it in place.

9. Align the hemmed edges of the four end pieces with the edges of the box around the lid opening. Pin the pieces, wrong side uppermost, to the

rectangular piece of silk already in place, matching the raw edges.

10. Carefully remove the silk cover from the box and machine or hand stitch the pinned seams.

11. Turn the cover the right side out and slip it over the box once more, easing it into the correct

position. Catch with a few neat stitches through the silk into the interlining beneath, at the edges and corners of the box, some of which will be hidden by braid.

12. Glue lengths of braid around the edges of the body of the box and the lid, which will help keep the silk taut and in place. Glue

1. If you intend using paint rather than silk inside the hatbox, apply two coats of green emulsion using a small paint-brush. Allow the first coat to dry before applying the second. Leave to dry.

2. To calculate the quantity of silk required to cover the lid, measure the depth of the lid side and double it to take into account the inside of the lid. Add another good ½in (1.5cm) to allow for sticking the raw edge to the inside base of the lid beneath the circle of silk that will line the lid.

3. Place the fabric wrong side uppermost and stand the lid on top. Measure outwards from the lid to include the measurement you have just taken. Mark out the larger circle on the fabric using a pencil and cut out the fabric.

4. Lay the box lid on more of the fabric, again wrong side uppermost, and mark then cut out a circle ½in (1.5cm) larger than the exact lid size – this is for the inside of the lid.

5. To calculate the size of the silk band required to cover the side of the box, measure the height of the box and double it, as before, to allow for covering the inside of the box. Add another 2in (5cm) to this measurement – allowing for 1in (2.5cm) to tuck under the circle that will line the base inside, and 1in (2.5cm) to tuck under the circle covering the underneath of the box outside. Also measure the circumference of the box and

add 1in (2.5cm) to allow for the side seam.

6. To cut out the circle of silk required to cover the base of the box, have the fabric wrong side uppermost and place the box on top. Again, mark the outline on the fabric and cut a good ½in (1.5cm) outside the marked circle to allow for turning under the raw edge.

7. Press all the pieces of silk you have cut out.

8. Lay the large circle of silk for the outside of the lid in front of you, wrong side uppermost. Place the lid upside down in the centre of the fabric. Bring the silk up over the edge of the lid to the inside, using clothes pegs or small bulldog clips to hold it in place temporarily. Continue around the lid – you may have to make little pleats occasionally to keep the fabric taut.

9. Hot glue the silk to the inside edge of the box, pulling it tight as you work gradually around the lid. The raw edge of the silk can be left unfinished on the inside since it will eventually be covered. Leave until the hot glue is dry, i.e. it is cold and no longer sticky.

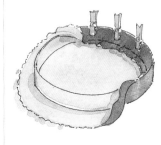

10. Take the circle of silk for the inside of the lid and turn the edge under evenly all round by ½in (1.5cm) so that it will fit the inside of the lid exactly. Pin then stitch the turned hem, before hot gluing the piece into position on the inside of the lid, covering the raw edge of the first piece of silk.

11. With right sides facing, pin together the ends of the large rectangle of silk that will cover the side of the box. Stitch then press the seam open. Turn the band the right side out and slip it over the box, leaving about 1in (2.5cm) of fabric overhanging the bottom of the box. Fold this over the base of the box and hot glue in place.

12. Once the glue is dry, smooth the fabric up the sides of the box and fold it over the rim to the inside of the box. Again, use clothes pegs to keep the silk taut; hot glue the silk to the base inside the box. As on the lid, the raw edge is acceptable as it will be covered.

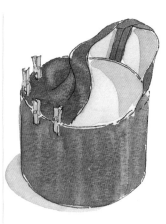

13. Turn under the edge of the silk circle for the inside of the box, just as you did for the piece for the inside of the lid. Pin then stitch. Place the hemmed circle inside the box and carefully stick over the raw edge of the main piece of silk, using fabric glue which should not come through and mark the silk.

14. Cut the ribbon into two generous lengths – you will need much more than you would imagine for an extravagantly sumptuous look! Neaten the two ends and attach to the inside edge of the lid, opposite one another, with glue. Replace the lid and tie the ribbon into a fabulous bow, teasing the wired edges into an attractive shape.

15. Finally, hot glue gold sequins all around the side of the box, taking great care not to burn your fingers.

FUCHSIA PINK SILK BOX

You will need

Sturdy card/papier mâché
*   round box*
Small paintbrush
Matt emulsion paint in a pink
*   to match the silk*
Pencil
Tape measure
Sharp scissors
Padded curtain interlining
Fabric glue
Pink pure silk
Iron
Long glass-headed pins
Sewing machine or needle
*   and thread*
Long lengths of sequin ribbon
*   in two colours*

1. Paint the inside of the box and the very top of the outside, which will not be covered with silk, with pink matt emulsion. Allow the first coat to dry before applying a second. Leave to dry.

2. With the lid in place, pencil a line around the box against the edge of the lid. This denotes where the fabric must start otherwise the lid is unlikely to fit.

3. Start by covering the box with the interlining. As before, there is no need to allow extra for turning the raw edges. To calculate the quantity of interlining needed to run around the outside of the box, determine the width of the piece by measuring from just below the pencil line down to the bottom of the box only, and the length by measuring the circumference of the box. Stick the band

on to the box using fabric glue. To determine the interlining needed for the box base and lid top, stand the box then the lid on the interlining and cut exactly to size. Stick these pieces in place. Finally, cut a strip of interlining for the side of the lid, its length equal to the circumference of the lid and its width fractionally less than the lid depth. Stick in place.

4. To calculate the size of the silk band to run around the outside of the box, measure the outside depth of the box from the pencil line to the base of the box and measure the circumference of the box. Add a good ½in (1.5cm) to each edge to allow for the seams and for turning under the raw edge along the top of the cover, since silk frays badly.

5. To measure the silk required to cover the base of the box, place the fabric wrong side up and stand the box on top. Using a pencil, mark the base of the box on the fabric. Cut a good ½in (1.5cm) outside the marked shape to allow for the seam.

6. To calculate the amount of silk required for the top of the lid, lay the lid on the fabric as before. Again, mark the outline on the fabric and cut a good ½in (1.5cm) outside the marked circle to allow for the seam.

7. Finally, cut a strip of silk for the side of the lid. Measure the outside depth of the lid and the circumference, and add an extra ½in (1.5cm) to each edge to allow for the seams and for turning under the raw edge on the bottom edge of the lid as before.

8. Cut three more long strips to the same length, this time cutting them on the bias, and making them about 1in (2.5cm) wide. Two are for "double-cording" the edge of the lid, the third piece for twisting into a "rose" for decoration. (This is optional as braid could be used instead.)

9. Press all the pieces of silk. Take the rectangle of silk for the body of the box. Neatly hem the long edge that will fit flush against the edge of the lid, by turning it under twice, pinning then machine or hand stitching. Wrap this hemmed piece of silk in position around the side of the box with the wrong side facing out. Pin the side seam formed where the two ends of silk meet. Push a couple of pins through into the interlining to hold the rest of the band in place.

10. Place the piece of silk for the bottom of the box right side up. Place the silk-covered box on top. Pin the two pieces of silk together around the base of the box. Remove the pinned silk from the box to first baste (tack) then stitch the seam. At intervals around the seam carefully snip across the raw edges as far as the stitching, at an angle to the sewing line. This helps ease the silk into shape and avoid puckering.

11. Following the directions in Step 9, hem one long edge of the narrow length of silk for the edge of the lid. Wrap the strip around the lid, the wrong side facing out, with the hemmed edge of silk flush with the bottom edge of the lid. Pin the side seam formed where the two ends of silk meet.

12. Place the remaining piece of silk on top of the lid, wrong side uppermost. Pin the silk accurately to the narrow side piece. As before, remove the pinned silk from the lid to first baste (tack) then stitch together. Again, make small angled cuts around the stitching to help prevent the silk from puckering.

13. Turn both covers to the right side and press.

14. Slip the cover on to the base of the box and attach it to the glued interlining with a few tiny stitches around the bottom edge of the box and at the side seam. If the cover seems loose, insert a little glue very carefully under the top edge of the cover. Fit the cover on the lid in the same way.

15. To make the flat silk trim and the rose, take the three strips of silk cut on the bias, turn under the long raw edges on each to meet in the middle of the strip and press flat. Press under the raw edges at the end of each strip. Carefully glue two of the strips around the side of the box lid, one below the other. Hold in place with pins stuck into the interlining until the glue dries.

16. To make the rose for the side of the lid, coil and twist the third strip of pressed silk into a rose shape, sewing it at the back with firm stitches. Stick it on top of the ends of the glued strips, holding it in place with pins until the glue dries.

17. Finally, stick lengths of sequin ribbon on the top of the lid with fabric glue.

Gifts for men

A stylish paper bin, sponged in a Christmassy red and decorated with hand-painted leaves, makes a most acceptable and highly fashionable gift for most men, as does an attractively shaped and decorated bottle holder for holding a favourite bottle of wine.

LEAF-PAINTED WASTE PAPER BIN

You will need

Tin waste paper bin
1in (2.5 cm) household paintbrush
Matt emulsion paint in red
Old spoon
PVA glue
Clean plastic carton with lid
Artist's acrylic tube paint in Payne's grey, white and gold, plus raw umber (optional)
Natural sea sponge
Kitchen paper
Pair of lightweight disposable gloves
White chalk
Jam jar
Nos. 5 or 6 and 3 or 4 artist's paintbrushes
Decorator's acrylic semi-matt varnish

Tinware, like this waste paper bin and the wine bottle holders overleaf, comes already oxidized. For the bin, choose emulsion paint in a shade of red within the terracotta to scarlet hues, as opposed to pinky red. You may find it helpful to practise painting the leaves on paper before you start on the bin (see overleaf).

1. Paint the bin inside and out, and underneath, with the red emulsion paint, allowing the first coat to dry before applying a second. If the paint resists or separates, add a drop or two of washing-up liquid to the paint to make it adhere. Leave to dry.

2. Mix a spoonful of the red emulsion paint with a spoonful of PVA glue and up to four parts water in a plastic carton to make a glaze. Squeeze a little Payne's grey tube paint on to the lid of the carton, using it as a palette. Replenish the paint if necessary as you work.

3. Squeeze out the sea sponge in clean water then squeeze it a second time in kitchen paper to remove excess water.

4. Wearing disposable gloves, dip the tip of the sponge into the red glaze, then into the Payne's grey on the carton lid. Dab it on to the surface of the bin and begin sponging diagonally. Continue until the whole surface has a slightly marbled look – stop before it becomes muddy and all the same colour. If you need to, you can bring the colour back to

red again by dipping the sponge in the glaze first, then into the tin of neat red paint. Experiment until you have the finish you want. Leave to dry. (Wash out the sponge well afterwards, or the PVA glue will turn it rock hard!)

5. Before painting the leaves on the bin, first mark the direction of each one using white chalk. Alter any chalk marks if necessary by wiping with damp kitchen paper, until you are satisfied with the pattern.

6. Fill a jam jar with water. Squeeze a little Payne's grey and a little white tube paint on to a clean palette. Wet the no. 5 or 6 artist's paintbrush with water, then dip one side of the brush into the grey paint and the other

into the white. Paint each leaf (see the feather pictures above, which show the same technique), working from the base of the leaf to its tip. When all the leaves are completed, leave to dry.

7. Using the gold tube paint and the no. 3 or 4 paintbrush, highlight the centre of each leaf, then outline each with gold.

8. Using the gold paint and the same paintbrush, paint along the top edge of the bin to highlight the attractive fluted top. You will need to apply two or three coats to achieve a dense finish that eradicates the brush marks. (If you prefer an antique gold colour, mix the gold with a little raw umber tube paint.) Leave to dry thoroughly.

9. To finish the bin, seal the paintwork inside and out with two coats of decorator's acrylic semi-matt varnish, applied with a clean household paintbrush. Take great care when varnishing to brush upwards to avoid drips and runs occurring around the fluted top. Allow the first coat to dry completely before applying the second. The outside will take about 1 hour to dry, but the inside of the bin will take longer.

WINE BOTTLE HOLDER

You will need

Tin wine bottle holders
½in (1.5cm) household
    paintbrush
Matt emulsion paint in
    dark brown
Washing-up liquid
Old spoon
PVA glue
Plastic carton with lid
Artist's acrylic tube paint in
    Payne's grey or black,
    white and rich gold, plus
    cadmium red or orange
    (optional)
Natural sea sponge
Kitchen paper
Pair of lightweight disposable
    gloves
White chalk
Jam jar
No. 4 artist's paintbrush
Decorator's acrylic semi-matt
    varnish

Attractively shaped containers such as these have many uses, other than as wine bottle holders. They make ideal planters and useful desk "tidies" for pens and pencils. They are also perfect for holding fat church candles, surrounded by dry oasis packed

snugly into the pots and sprinkled with star anise or tiny larch cones, which have been sprayed gold to pick up the gold paint of the painted feathers.

1. Paint the holders inside and out, and underneath, with the dark brown emulsion paint, allowing the first coat to dry, before applying a second. (Use a little washing-up liquid if necessary, as on page 129.)

2. Make up the emulsion glaze as before by mixing a spoonful of PVA glue and a spoonful of brown emulsion with up to four parts water in a plastic carton. Squeeze a little Payne's grey or black tube paint on to the carton lid palette, followed by a little raw umber and a tiny amount of red or orange, if using.

3. Squeeze out the sponge in clean water then squeeze it a second time in kitchen paper to remove excess water.

4. Wearing disposable gloves, dip the tip of the sponge into the glaze, then into the Payne's grey or black on the carton lid. Dab it on to the surface of each holder, sponging as before. When you need to replenish the paint on

the sponge, dip it into the glaze first, as before, then into a little red or orange, if using. Continue sponging over the holders, inside and out, in this way until you are satisfied with the finish. Leave to dry. (Wash out the sponge well afterwards, or the PVA glue will turn it rock hard!)

5. For the feather design use a piece of white chalk to draw the outline of the three feathers on the side of each holder to ensure a balanced design.

6. Using the Payne's grey and white tube paints with a little water and a no. 4 artist's paint-brush, paint the feathers in the same way as you did the leaves on the waste bin (see Step 6). Highlight one side of each feather in white or paler grey. When dry, highlight the centre of each feather with rich gold tube paint. Leave to dry.

7. Finish the wine bottle holder as for the bin by painting two or three coats of rich gold tube paint along the fluted edges of the holders. Leave to dry thoroughly then seal the paint-work, inside and out, with two coats of decorator's acrylic semi-matt varnish (see Steps 8– 9).

Ingenious ideas

Attention to detail helps make any occasion more memorable and the Christmas table is no exception. Use crackers, candles, floral arrangements, tree decorations and gold and silver trimmings to achieve your chosen look. Similarly, when putting up the Christmas decorations and wrapping your presents for the tree, don't forget the container for the Christmas tree needs decorating, too! Plenty of inspiration follows...

Festive tables

Decorating the Christmas table requires as much attention to detail as preparing the food. Your table centre may be as spontaneous as a group of candles standing on a plate surrounded by ivy, or glass baubles in a sparkling glass dish, or it may be something elaborate and breathtaking!

PURPLE & GOLD

A combination of purple, gold, white and green predominates in the colour scheme used in the decorations for this table, which is laid for the celebration meal. Reflected candlelight provides an extra warmth; gold catches the light providing an added richness, while greenery from the garden or collected from a nearby wood or hedgerow provides the traditional evergreen colour of the season.

For centuries, holly and ivy have been brought into the house at Christmas time to protect the house and the family within. Certainly, the holly and ivy wreaths that adorn our front doors are not a florist's invention, but an ancient tradition founded on our ancestors' belief in their magic powers of protection against evil spirits, lightning and other evils.

To achieve a look similar to this one, cover the table with a white damask cloth. Arrange a long piece of butter muslin over the cloth in swags around the top, loosely knotting it at intervals. Decorate these knots with lengths of trailing ivy coiled into circles, their ends twisted a

few times to hold them in place. Tie antique linen napkins with beautifully embroidered sari braid edged in gold. Scatter pressed dried leaves, sprayed with gold metallic spray paint (see page 16), together with dragees and other decorative gold objects over the table. Finally, present small gifts for each table setting in sari braid treasure bags (see page 26).

THE FLORAL CANDLE ARRANGEMENTS

These arrangements in their purple pots are truly stunning. Originally shallow terracotta plant pots of the type easily available at garden centres or DIY outlets, the pots have been painted with purple matt emulsion paint, then sponged with a water-based emulsion glaze applied with a natural sea sponge. To make similar floral arrangements line the pots with plastic to prevent water from the pieces of tightly packed presoaked wet oasis seeping through the porous terracotta. If using large church candles it is best to tape florist's wire "hairpins" around their bases, before pushing them deep into the wet oasis. This method is far firmer

and much safer than pushing the actual candle into the oasis, or cutting a hole for it, as it will inevitably wobble!

Since the choice of flowers may be limited at Christmas, a good selection of evergreens, such as hebe, viburnum, bay or camellia leaves, is important for filling the pot. You could also intersperse silk ribbon roses (see page 14) throughout the arrangement for added colour and interest.

BLUE, SILVER & WHITE BUFFET TABLE

Cover the table with a bedspread, dyed linen sheet, colourful curtain or rug of whatever colour you choose for your party table.

Here, blue was the obvious choice to offset the Spanish handmade pottery and other china and an antique French linen sheet was successfully dyed in the washing machine.

Tie lengths of silver wire-edged ribbon into bows and pin them to the cloth on the four sides of the table. The silver of the ribbon adds sparkle to the setting, as does the use of silver-sprayed walnuts, seed heads and autumn leaves, and silver dragees which can all be scattered on the tablecloth.

Wrap blue metallic ribbon around the linen napkins and tie silver sari braid over the top. Complete the three-coloured theme with silver and white handmade crackers (see page 94), decorated with silver-sprayed echinops and larch cones.

Once the buffet table is set, light all the candles and uncork the champagne or bring in the mulled wine!

LOW-LEVEL TABLE

If you prefer to sit on the floor and eat from a low table, or simply to use a coffee table for an informal supper, you can still decide on an atmosphere or theme on which to build.

Decorative grouping has the most impact – the trick is being able to recognize items in your home and using them in an impromptu and pleasing way. Look at all the things around you and gather together pieces of the same colour or shape.

Here, a wonderful silk Indian sari with richly embroidered braid in perfect seasonal colours is used as a tablecloth. Paint wine glasses with red and green glass paints (see pages 105–7), and make gilded paper giftbags (see page 18) to add to the richness of the theme.

Use fresh red and green peppers to hold scented hand-made natural beeswax candles. Lastly, use a small cinnamon basket (see page 83) to hold evocatively scented Christmas pot-pourri, and use red tea lights and votive candles to echo the whole low-level scheme.

Imaginative Christmas tree containers

Every year, life seems to become more and more hectic, time begins to run out on the countdown to the big day and you may not have given any thought as to how you intend to display the Christmas tree. Consider, too, the type of Christmas tree you want and how to look after it

SELECTING THE TREE

Living in east Dorset, close to the New Forest, we are surrounded by both ancient forests and commercial Christmas tree plantations. The traditional Christmas tree found in most homes in the UK is the Norway spruce, which unfortunately is prone to losing its needles. A few of the specialist growers treat their trees, which helps to prevent needle drop. This year why not plan ahead and take a trip into the countryside to visit one of the specialist growers? You can be certain to find only the freshest Christmas trees cut on a weekly or even daily basis to restock the sales outlet.

You can choose from several species of Christmas tree in a huge variety of sizes, ranging from 2ft (0.6m) to 10–12ft (3–3.6m), and you will be able to stand back and look at the tree's shape, form and colour before making your final choice. Once you have made a decision, the tree will be sleeved for you,

which makes it easier to transport it home. Larger trees – those above 10ft (3m) – usually need to be ordered in advance.

The worst option is to buy a tree from a supermarket or high street shop (other than a florist's) which is already netted or sleeved in polythene, as it is then impossible to judge the quality or the shape of the tree.

Needlefast trees include Nordman, Noble fir and Scots pine, the latter being indigenous to the UK. The more unusual or difficult-to-find trees are Grandice and Frazer fir – both also grown in the UK. Trees in this needlefast and unusual group have a quite different appearance – their needles are blue-green or silver-green.

The Noble fir is indeed a noble-looking tree, with beautiful silver grey-green needles and evenly spaced whorls. The trees are not usually cut until at least 8ft (2.5m) tall and are a great deal more expensive because they take longer to grow. The Scots pine has particularly long needles

– if your decorations are small you will have great difficulty fixing them on the branches.

Remember to water the tree if at all possible. It was once a living thing and its sap will only nourish it for a short time. Many Christmas tree outlets sell purpose-made tree stands, which hold water, where the tree trunk can be clamped between "teeth" by standing on a pedal or lever.

If, like me, you consider it wasteful to cut a living tree to use for only a week or so before discarding it, order a container-grown tree. Such trees can be brought into the house annually – for a few years at least – before they become too large and have to be planted out in the garden. Do remember to water a container-grown tree generously.

CONTAINER OPTIONS

So often I can remember a last-minute performance of whittling the bottom off a thick tree with an inadequate knife, trying to

avoid touching the needles, to which I am allergic, and the sap from the stem, while attempting to ram it into a narrow tree-stand, which was far too light-weight to support a tall tree anyway! It was so unstable we had to wire it to a curtain rail and the radiator as the cat took great pleasure in jumping up at the decorations, which brought the tree forward to lean at a very dangerous angle, only saved by a high-backed dining chair!

Toddlers are fascinated by the lights and glittering decorations as well as animals, so it is as well to consider how the tree is to be contained. Here are a few ideas to help you mask the inevitable soil- or stone-filled bucket with something other than a last-minute bit of crêpe paper.

SEASONAL COLOURED CLOTH

Drape a large tall basket with seasonal red and white thick cotton cloth in a swagged fashion and knot it at the side – a very effective look that takes only minutes to achieve.

JUTE HESSIAN

Use jute hessian to cover an old bucket. The lovely earthy colour and natural fibres combine wonderfully with the tassel from a curtain tie-back, also made from jute. Twist a long narrow strip of hessian around the top of the bucket as shown or use anything in the same colour, such as a clothes line made from natural fibres or a short piece of rope, which would look just as attractive.

VICTORIAN-STYLE PAPER

Fill a tall Edwardian bucket with soil to house your tree. Wind a piece of strong wire around the stem in line with the top of the bucket, and wrap the ends of the wire around the top of the bucket, just under the top rim, to keep it centred and stable.

Pleat two sheets of Victorian-style paper to fit the shape of the bucket. Use masking tape to hold the pleats in position inside the top and underneath the bucket, and around the side of the bucket at the back out of sight.

WHITE & GOLD

Check the shed or garden for any
suitable tree containers. This one was
probably once the lining of an old coal
holder. Use good-quality, thick white
paper decorated with gold italic script
to cover the tin surface, and pretty it
up with a wide, wire-edged white and
gold ribbon tied in an attractive bow.

TERRACOTTA

Use a sizeable garden urn made from
plastic, but with a convincing terracotta finish. This one is large enough
to hold a large full tree, and to disguise
whatever packing you need to use
to anchor it.

ENAMELLED TIN

There are obviously more options for
containers for smaller Christmas trees.
Look around for any suitable kitchen-
ware. This old enamel bread bin, which
has been painted in sage green and
white, is perfect for a smaller tree, and
the chequered effect looks great in a
contemporary setting.

Directory of suppliers

The Bead Shop
21A Tower Street
London WC2H 9NS
Tel: 020-7240 0931

British Christmas Tree Growers Association
Tel: 0131-4470499
Website: www.bctga.org.uk

Calico Pie
15 Queen's Drive
Sedbergh
Cumbria LA10 5DP
Tel: 01539-620884
General craft supplier.
Mail order – free catalogue
and free p&p in UK.

Caspari Ltd
9 Shire Hill
Saffron Walden
Essex CB11 3AP
Tel: 01799-513010

Caxton Décor & Interiors
26–30 Salisbury Street
Fordingbridge
Hants SP6 1AF
Tel: 01425-653489
Huge range of paints and other
items, including DIY, sewing and
toy making materials. Trimmings
and braids, wonderful fabrics
with fast ordering service.
Stockists of Liberon and Polyvine
products (gilt creams etc.).

Craftworld
23–29 Queen Street
Belfast BT1 6EA
Tel: 01232-249000

Cranborne Woodlands
Christmas Tree Sales Outlet
The Fruit Farm
Alderholt
Fordingbridge
Hampshire
Tel: 01725-517289
To select your own superb quality
fresh trees.

Culpeper Ltd
21 Bruton Street
London W1X 7DA
For Culpeper mail order for
rosebuds, lavender and many
other herbs, tel: 01223-894054

Eaton's Seashells
30 Forest Drive West
London E11 1LA
Tel: 020-8539 5288
Mail order only. Sample
selection of shells available
for craft and collectors.

Falkiner Fine Papers
76 Southampton Row
London
WC1B 4AR
Tel: 020-7831 1151

Hobbycraft
Tel: 01202-596100
Arts and crafts superstores with
13 branches nationwide.

Homecrafts Direct
P O Box 38
Leicester LE1 9BU
Tel: 0161-251 3139
Mail order supplier – over 9,000
craft items. Catalogue available.

Ikea
Tel: 020-8208-5600
Lidded wooden box for White
Velvet Giftbox (see page 54)

Julia Gale Cake Decorations
53 The Borough
Downton
Salisbury
Wilts SP5 3LX
Telefax: 01725-513758
Everything for the professional
and amateur cake decorator, plus
fabulous ribbon – wide, wire-
edged and gossamer. Julia runs
regular courses and offers expert
advice to customers.

Lavenders of London
Unit 12, The Metro Centre
St John's Road
Isleworth
Middlesex TW7 6NJ
Tel: 020-8568 5733
Craft and florist's sundries.

Millers
28 Stockwell Street,
Glasgow G1 4RT
Tel: 0141-553 1660
Fine arts and crafts materials.

Panduro Hobby
Westway House
Transport Avenue
Brentford
Middlesex TW8 9HF
Tel: 020-8847 6161
Europe's largest mail order
supplier of craft/hobby products
– over 12,500 products.
Catalogue available.

Paperchase
213 Tottenham Court Road
London W1P 9AF
Tel: 020-7580 8496

Silkhance Fabrics
4 Tooting High Street
London SW17 0RG
Tel: 020-8682 1065
Mail order UK and overseas.
Fabulous silks, sari braids and
beaded braids, beautiful saris and
fabrics. Very friendly and helpful.

Smitcraft
Unit 1, Eastern Road
Aldershot
Hants GU12 4TE
Tel: 01252 342626
Mail order supplier of art,
craft and needlework materials.
Catalogue available.

Smiths Metal Centre
42–56 Tottenham Court Road
London N1 4BZ
Tel: 020-7241 1430
Suppliers of copper foil.

Stewart Stevenson
68 Clerkenwell Road
London EC1M 5QA
Tel: 020-7253 1693
Artists and gilding materials.

Index

Acknowledgements

This book is dedicated to Osh and Fianna with my fondest love, for restoring the magic of Christmas.

My special love and thanks must go to Marianne Grace (Maresie), a talented artist, designer, networker, confidante and dear friend, for her inspirational ideas and time-consuming work for many of the projects in the book.

I am indebted to the following people: Di Lewis, for her fabulous photography throughout the book; Penny Clarke for pulling out all the stops to transfer my typescript on to disk; Jo Lethaby, who must be the most patient, long-suffering and good-humoured editor anyone could possibly wish for. She even admitted she dreamt about this book! Thank you Jo for your encouragement; Nina Sharman, my commissioning editor at Hamlyn Octopus, with whom it is a pleasure to work; and Louise Griffiths, the senior designer.

My thanks to the following companies whose products enhanced the book: Caxton Décor & Interiors for all their help and advice; Caspari Limited, for their wonderful giftwrapping papers used in the Floral Giftwrapped Soaps project and Victorian-style Paper; and Earthworks for their beautiful handmade natural beeswax candles.